Books by Claudio Naranjo

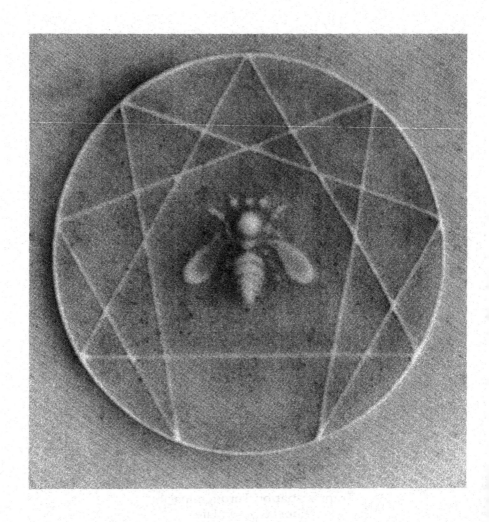

Enneagram and honey bee—symbols associated with the Sarmouni Order since ancient times. Picture of ceramic reproduced with kind permission of Stefan Maguire.

ENNEA-TYPE STRUCTURES

Self-Analysis for the Seeker

CLAUDIO NARANJO, M.D.

GATEWAYS/IDHHB, INC.
PUBLISHERS

Frontispiece photo by Slobodan Dan Paich.

The illustration, facing chapter title pages, are caricatures reproduced from chromolithographs published in *Vanity Fair* Magazine in London, during the late 19th century through 1914, when the magazine moved to New York.

The nine *Commedia dell'arte* characters illustrating the "Trait Structure" chapter sections were drawn by Kelly Rivera after original illustrations by Walter Massimelli for the book *Conoscere Le Machere Italiane* by Carla Poesio, ©1984 by Edizioni della Speranza s.r.l., Florence, Italy. These adaptations are used with kind permission of Edizioni Primavera s.a.s., Florence, Italy.

Illustrations to the "Existential Psychodynamics" section of each chapter are reproductions of original works by E.J. Gold, ©1990 by E.J Gold, used with the permission of the artist.

All illustrations were selected by the author as appropriate representations of the nine ennea-types described in this book. Figure VI on page 17 has been corrected from the first printing of this book.

"Protoanalysis" is a registered service mark of the Arica Institute, Inc.

First Printing: November, 1990.
Second Printing: February, 1991.
Third Printing: September, 1991.
Fourth Printing: April, 2004
Published by:
GATEWAYS/IDHHB, INC.
P.O. Box 370 Nevada City, CA 95959
(800) 869-0658 or (530) 477-8101

Library of Congress Cataloging-in-Publication Data
Naranjo, Claudio.
    Ennea-type structures : self-analysis for the seeker / Claudio Naranjo.
      p.   cm.
Includes bibliographical references.
ISBN: 0-89556-063-1 : $19.95
    1. Typology (Psychology) 2. Enneagram. 3. Self-evaluation.
    4. Personality assessment. I. Title.
      BF698-3.N37 1990   90-44320
      155.2/6—dc20   CIP

TABLE OF CONTENTS

Acknowledgement

This book would not have come to being without Oscar Ichazo, through whom I first became acquainted with the "enneagrams of personality" during a series of lectures dictated at the Instituto de Psicologia Aplicada (Santiago) in 1969, under the sponsorship of the Chilean Psychological Association—and who was later to be, more than a teacher, a spiritual midwife.

INTRODUCTION

by E.J. Gold

Claudio Naranjo is an accomplished therapist, a successful psychiatrist and professor who has acted for many years as a wonderful guide to pilgrims on the spiritual path. He is also the author of several valuable books in his field, the founder of the meteoric Seekers After Truth group in the Bay Area, a close associate of Oscar Ichazo, a protegé of the late Fritz Perls, an inheritor and shaper of the human potential movement, especially as practiced at the Esalen Institute and in Berkeley, California, and more recently a globe-trotting highly sought-after teacher and workshop leader. He is also for me a long-time friend and colleague whom I admire greatly.

This book is not a mere intellectual exercise. After working for decades on gathering the data supporting it, Claudio has at last decided to publish this penetrating study which culminates and synthesizes his lifetime of patient work—no pun intended. Over the years he has assembled a wealth of documentation, and this book presents the first facet of the results of his research. As he himself tells us, it is in fact the introduction to a much more detailed study that will be complete with erudite footnotes, abundant references, systematic analyses and clinical observations which will be intended primarily to reach the professional helper.

We are fortunate that Claudio has chosen this approach, for it allows a large body of readers to discover something that might otherwise have remained almost completely outside their grasp.

With this insightful typology readers both professional and lay now have the opportunity to discover Claudio Naranjo—if they haven't already—as a proponent of the enneagram teaching received from a little known Sufi school in the Middle East. I appreciate this endeavor and trust it will bear fruit in many unforeseen ways, not the least of which is to help bridge the gap between knowledge past and present.

By restricting the contents of this book to an outline of the types in the form of a working manual Claudio has created a sophisticated and useful handbook. There is no question that this is a very serious book, and yet I was able to enjoy and play with its contents, and I'm sure others will too, for its systematic qualities enable one to go from one chapter to another assessing where one sits in this round-table of ennea-types. I doubt that these ideas will ever make it to the parlor and become part of the social games the dilettantes of psychological ideas engage in, but there is hope that it will become a useful tool to the many who sincerely wish to know more about themselves and improve their self-knowledge.

What Claudio has accomplished here is no small feat. With all the tools of modern psychology he has taken a very ancient system—the enneagram—and given it a modern application. This is one of the reasons I find his work so exciting. He is neither dwelling on the past nor turning away from it but rather reuniting great intellectual discoveries spanning millenia. We're not talking about digging up old ideas just for the sake of nostalgia; we're looking at how these are just as valuable and pertinent today as they were then.

I wish to point out that, in my opinion, Claudio is too modest about himself and his own contributions. Throughout the years of his data collection he conducted many workshops exposing hundreds, perhaps thousands, of individuals to the ennea-type structures. Numerous activities of his enabled a few go-getters to incorporate these ideas into their own areas of research and thus help make the word "enneagram" more widely known. In a sense, he has fathered many studies and publications long before actually going public.

Claudio Naranjo has been a serious student of esoteric psychology and spirituality—serious to the point that his life has at times been unequivocally at risk for his convictions, a condition which to my knowledge never caused him to waver for a moment in his research and teaching work with others around him.

Is there possibly an inherent danger in the enneagram teaching? Is it a formulation so esoteric and exotic as to be instantly enlightening to students who contact it? My answer to the first question is resoundingly "yes," to the second "no."

The enneagram teaching which is becoming current, so much so that it's practically street knowledge, hardly seems dangerous in the popularized form. Like a refinement of sun-sign astrology, the once-esoteric imagery now provides thumb-nail sketches of the personality types that make it easy to "type oneself" and know just where one fits into the character system. This is material not so much for transformation as for titillation, more grist for the cocktail party mill, and the sales market.

Claudio's analysis of the types according to the enneagram is very different in its intention. It is done with unflinching candor and clarity: he lays bare underlying mechanisms of the human biological machine that are predictable and inescapable. He explains how we develop the binds that we find ourselves in as adults and what we can do about them, without limiting himself to the psychological point of view.

As human primates, we cannot avoid certain patterns of behavior; we cannot wish them away, ignore them, or easily transform them into virtues or mystical qualities. Claudio leaves no illusion about this. He is not proposing an instant cure but a means of looking at a profound problem and actually dealing with it. This is where he departs from any association with the seductive and destructive "new age" ideas that are so prevalent today. He stands apart from the insidious and ubiquitous illusions which surround and subvert great teachings into the service of the hypnotic sleep of primate existence.

Claudio does not mislead individuals into believing that a few psychological magic tricks will do the job for us. He does not hide the fact that the path of self-knowledge is indeed long and arduous, and no task for the lazy and superficial. Years of observation and conversations with him have clearly demonstrated to me that he does not partake of the homocentric philosophy of illusionism. While he may have a higher opinion than I do of the potential of humans "en masse," he does not commit the error for which I hold most proponents of the new psychology and psychiatry accountable, the misrepresentation of the transformational path as easy. However, what he does do for us is give us a tool that means something, that can actually help us achieve profound results.

Most psychological systems blot out a higher spiritual life, engulfing it in a never-ending wave-cancellation doublethink that reduces spirituality to mere brain games. In my opinion, one of the most valuable aspects of Claudio's contribution is that he allows psychology to serve a higher spiritual purpose. Claudio leaves room for the spiritual life and distinguishes quite correctly the nature of the psychological realm from the spiritual realm which is rarely the case with psychologists who recognize the spiritual dimension but usually reduce it to psychological terms. Claudio makes no attempt to appropriate this domain. For those who are inclined to follow the path of self-analysis and examination, this material affords a unique opportunity to actually prepare oneself for a life in the Work. Few psychological systems can say this about themselves.

The reader of this book will find the language straightforward and precise without being overly academic. The analysis itself is highly detailed and utterly professional. The format employed by the author makes for easy use; important character traits are either in bold type or in quotation marks enabling an easy recognition of key phrases for practitioners who will use this as a technical manual. For the lay person a background in psychology is not necessary to grasp the fundamental outlines that are sketched for us by Claudio's systematic description of the types.

But more than that, Claudio has hit the bullseye when he roots his analysis in the grounding statement that *all the ennea-types* are variations of the human malaise of "ontic obscuration" which translates as "loss of Being." This concept alone makes the book worth reading. Because of it I cannot recommend strongly enough to any serious student of psychology the reading of this book. It is crucial to a correct understanding of the hierarchy of domains between Being and personality which we must address on any path of inner life.

If we understand the point at which a change in behavior begins to appear as a means of filling the sense of emptiness—this vacuity of Being, this inner loss—of disguising the obscuration, then we can already begin to look at lifelong patterns of behavior in a different way and thus free ourselves a little from some of the weights which bind us to this planet. This simple and elegant concept provides a rare tool for seeing the etiology of neurosis, psychosis, or, in another language, sleep, how we go from a state of openness and awakening as children to a state of dullness and atrophy as adults.

The concept of "ontic obscuration" has many names in the various esoteric traditions, but it is always present in any truthful psychology of Being. It corresponds roughly to the essential self's identification with the sleep of the machine; although the Being or essence does not sleep, it agrees to permit itself to be hypnotised, or become seduced by the attraction of something about the life of human primates with their various ennea-types and corresponding ennea-pursuits and ennea-pleasures.

As to the second issue, the potency of this teaching, well... what is it worth to you, personally? There is no magic *in the system itself*. Like any genuine teaching, it works for you only if you do the work. I have delved deeply into the enneagram and used it myself, for my own inquiries and in working with others. The geometric figure is the equivalent of other figures in other teachings: the star of David, the tree of life, the major arcana of the Tarot, archetypal characters and divinities, and so forth. In a sense, the figures and systems they refer to are arbitrary, and coherent within themselves. Choice of one system over another is usually just a question of preference based on immediate working applications.

What is esoteric about this teaching, in the sense of hidden or secret, is the *appropriate use* of the knowledge. This you must learn from a practitioner who knows, who is initiated, or from guides that manifest in macro-dimensional chambers. One who knows the use of such a system for the separation of machine from essence is free to modify and adapt that system. Claudio has thoroughly explored and domesticated this enneagram system and ingeniously adapted it for use in this psychologically sophisticated culture. His credentials are first-rate and his knowledge is not the cheap sort, simply learned from books or speculation. He has worked with this system for years, and he knows its uses and abuses.

Readers should beware of the limitations of any system; they should trust only the intuitional sense of the essential self, not be led astray by iron pyrite, and accept only the real treasure that is in the guarded cave, at the end of a rainbow, or in a leprechaun's cache. They should also remember that one's ennea-type can not only walk and talk and interact socially with others; it can also study and meditate and perform practices and experience ecstasies, visions or mystical unions.

If *Ennea-Type Structures* can further the reader's enterprise of discernment and nurture the essence-life in any way, then Claudio has made another contribution to the benefit of all sentient beings—and I, for one, thank him.

xv

AUTHOR'S FOREWORD

Sometime in 1987, as I was passing through my native country, my friend Marta Huepe, who had been my host and heard about my various projects, invited me to return to her home at some future date to produce this book with her writing assistance. I took her up on this offer during January and February of 1988, and I dictated into a cassette recorder a book which I first thought of calling *Character Structure and Psychodynamics in the Light of the Enneagram of the Sarmouni* and which, after finishing, I renamed—more simply and yet more ambitiously—*Neurosis and Character in the Light of the Enneagram.*

The ease with which the book came into the world was not matched by the obstructions and toils surrounding its completion. Marta, driven by a combination of enthusiasm for the book's content, personal devotion and a lifelong habit of zeal, worked long hours and almost managed to type into my portable computer all the recorded material that I produced day after day. Only a few tapes were left to complete after my departure, but as her summer holidays ended, her ten year old daughter returned from Mexico, and other complications descended upon her life; these few cassettes remained untranscribed for months.

xvii

I will spare my readers the odyssey of the various accidents and difficulties that caused the book to remain unfinished in the course of the next year. Even when I came to Chile again in early 1989 with the intention of editing the manuscript, all manner of difficulties stood in the way of completing the task. Last but not least, the work accomplished was considerably maimed when, returning from South America, my hand bag—containing part of the manuscript—was stolen at the San Francisco airport.

Whether all this has been accident, the intervention of God's unfathomable will, demonic interference, or all of the above I don't know, yet I feel pleased, for I think it has been good for the book. The loss of the psychodynamic maps and trait lists in particular (implying the need to omit the references to them and to give up the hope of completing the task until a next writing vacation) served as a background for a new publishing idea that not only accommodates my circumstances, but, I think, provides a more fitting vehicle for the book's emergence into the world: that of dividing the volume into two distinct publications, of which this is the first.[1]

The stimulus for the idea of publishing the present portion of *Neurosis and Character in the Light of the Enneagram* was a visit to E.J. Gold, shortly before leaving for Andalucia, where I'm now setting out to extract and edit that part of the book containing the conceptual elaboration of my cumulative personal observations on the nine ennea-types over nearly twenty years and the spelling out of the psychodynamic reflections upon each. I am using the expression "ennea-type," of course, as a short equivalent for ego-type or character type according to the enneagram.

[1] I have extracted here what is most relevant to the book's immediate user (that is to say, the seeker) while I leave for the complete volume the more scholarly portions that will be of interest to psychotherapists and personality theorists.

The psychological characteristics described in each of the chapters under the heading of "Trait Structure" are the result of research comprising various stages:

1. The elaboration of lists of character descriptors based upon my cumulative experience.
2. A conceptual clustering of traits so as to generate groups of descriptors that can serve as pointers to the more generalized traits.
3. Psychodynamic maps geometrically representing clinically observed or inferred relationships among generalized traits. Though the graphics of these models (together with lists and cluster charts) were lost, some of the dynamic relations indicated in them are echoed in the writing.

Although many of these observations have become known indirectly through the teaching activity of my former students and the books of some who studied with them, I not only fail to agree fully with the statements published thus far but—now that secrecy concerning the enneagram has been broken by them—I have felt drawn to state my experience in my own way.

Also, going beyond mere strings of traits, as I did when formulating the first descriptions of the character types during my teaching experience in the early 70's, I am here focusing on how these descriptors are organized in terms of underlying traits and motives, and I also elaborate throughout the chapters of the book upon a theory of neurosis that differs from Freudian libido theory and only partially coincides with the object relations view: an existential interpretation of neurosis according to which the bottom line of all psychopathology is the loss of being (i.e., the absence of the direct experience or cognition of being) that theologians have called ignorance.

I have called this the Nasruddin Theory of Neurosis, in reference to the famous joke about the Mullah, according to which he was once on all fours looking for something in one of the alleys at the market place. A friend—as is well known—joined him in the search for what, as the Mullah explained to him, was the very key to his house. Only after a long time had elapsed without bringing success did the friend think of asking him, "Are you sure that you've lost it here?" To which Nasruddin replied, "No, I'm sure I lost it at home." "Then why are you looking for it here?" "There is much more light here," explained the Mullah.

The central idea underlying this book, then, is that we are looking for the key to our liberation, to our ultimate fulfillment, in the wrong place, and that this cognitive error is at the source of our dissatisfactions.

Throughout these pages I call this key "being," though it could be justly said that to give it even that name is too limited and limiting. We may say that we are, but we don't have the experience of being; we don't *know* that we are. On the contrary, the closer the scrutiny to which we subject our experience, the more we discover, at its core, a sense of lack, an emptiness, insubstantiality, a lack of selfness or being. From a lack of perceived sense of being—it is my contention— derives *deficiency motivation*, the basic oral drive that sustains the whole libido tree. But libido is not Eros, as Freud proposed. Eros is abundance, and deficiency is the search for abundance, which takes as many forms as the ruling passions that, according to this theory, constitute the lower emotional center.

The systematic examination—on the basis of these clusters—of how in each ennea-type the trait tree is supported by a dyadic central system of root traits[2] that sustains and is in turn sustained by ontic obscuration, may be considered both the empirical corroboration of a traditional view and a contribution to the self-understanding of those moved to use this book as a tool for self-study.

[2]Identifiable as the root passion and fixation.

ENNEA-TYPE STRUCTURES
Self-Analysis for the Seeker

BY WAY OF INTRODUCTION
A THEORY OF PERSONALITY

Oscar Ichazo frequently used the expression "this theory" notwithstanding the fact that he regarded the view of the psyche that he presented as an objective knowledge originally arrived at through revelation. Yet even if the more awakened may have grasped these ideas intuitively and experientially rather than experimentally, the word "theory" seems appropriate if we use it not in today's scientific sense of a hypothetic construction, but in the original meaning of the Greek *theoria:* vision.

In the following pages I will undertake to outline the vision in a broad way—and not necessarily in the terms in which I heard it presented. Throughout this book I will sometimes use, as Ichazo did, the word "Protoanalysis," to describe it, though this term makes reference not only to a body of knowledge, but primarily to a process of self-inquiry.[1]

---

[1] In this teaching, Protoanalysis constitutes the first stage in a process comprising the application of three successive methods. Beyond work of self-observation and confrontation which has self-insight as its goal, the work proceeds to a "holy war" against the ego in which efforts are made to inhibit the compulsive aspects of the personality and to cultivate the virtue corresponding to the individual's ruling passion. The third stage is of a contemplative nature, and is geared to an experiential understanding (through sophisticated techniques of meditation with an object) of the "Holy Ideas": aspects of reality that have the virtue of dissolving the individual's fixation or implicit cognitive error.

The broadest distinction in this body of Fourth Way psychology that I seek to outline is one between what Gurdjieff called "essence" and what he called "personality"—between the real being and the conditioned being with which we ordinarily identify. Where Gurdjieff spoke of personality, Ichazo spoke of ego—more in line with recent usage (ego trip, ego death, ego transcendence, and so on) than with the meaning given to "ego" in today's ego-psychology. The distinction is similar to that proposed today by Winnicott between the "real self" and the "false self," yet it may be misleading to speak of essence, soul, true self or atman as if their reference were something fixed and identifiable. Rather than speak of essence as a thing, then, we should think of it as a process, an ego-less, unobscured and free manner of *functioning* of the integrated human wholeness.

Though "ego" is the word I most often used while presenting these ideas in the early seventies, in this book I expect to be using at least as often the word "character," which I consider an appropriate equivalent for the same notion without the disadvantage of a clash with the meaning of "ego" in modern psychoanalysis.

A derivative from the Greek *charaxo* meaning to engrave, "character" makes reference to what is constant in a person, because it has been engraved upon one, and thus to behavioral, emotional and cognitive conditionings. It has been one of the merits of contemporary psychology to elucidate the process of the deterioration of consciousness in early life as a consequence of early emotional frustration in the family context.

In reaction to pain and anxiety, the individual seeks to cope with a seeming emergency through a corresponding emergency response ·that, precisely in virtue of the perceived survival threat, becomes fixed, becoming a repetition compulsion, as Freud called it.

This is a process that entails a loss of contact with all but the emergency foreground of experience (a dimming of consciousness) and at the same time an automatization, through which the person becomes to some extent a robot rather than a free agent in his life.

Together with the dimming of consciousness and automatization that set in in response to early pain, there is in the structure of the ego a polarity of over-desiring and hatred that, along with consciousness obscuration, have been emphasized in Buddhist doctrine as the three poisons underlying samsaric existence, i.e., three roots of egoic consciousness.

The theory of neurosis implicit in the Protoanalytic view is congruent with the Freudian and Reichian views of neurosis as a consequence of a curtailment of instinct, and also with the conception of health as unobstructed self-regulation generally shared by humanistic psychologists since Rogers and Perls. Though instinct theory has gone out of fashion in psychoanalytic circles since the rise of ethology, the present psychological theory acknowledges the pervasiveness of three goals in human behavior: survival, pleasure and relationships.[2]

It is asserted that individuals usually experience an imbalance in regard to the dominant instinct, and part of the work has to do with its correction. Such an imbalance is understood as a result of an invasion of the instinctual sphere by an egoic factor—which is represented in the Protoanalytic map as a displacement of a passion from the lower emotional center to one of the instinctual sub-centers.

Unlike traditional religions, which implicitly equate the instinctual with the sphere of the passions, the

---

[2] Though Marx's interpretation of human life emphasized hunger, Freud emphasized sex, and present day object-relations theorists emphasize affection, I do not think that anybody has embraced a view that integrates these three fundamental drives.

present view of the mind which conceives the healthy and optimal state as one of free or liberated instinct, could be adequately equated with the contemporary notion of self-regulation. It is a view in which the true enemy in the Holy War that the Fourth Way heritage prescribes against the false or lower self is not the animal within, but the realm of passionate drives that contaminate, repress and stand in place of instinct—and also, most decisively, the cognitive aspects of the ego, "fixations," which in turn sustain the passions.

While it is a goal of this tradition of work-on-self to bring about a shift in the control of behavior from the lower emotional center of the passions to a higher center, a still further stage is envisioned: a shift from the lower intellectual center of ordinary cognition—pervaded by wrong views of reality formed in child-hood (fixations)—to the higher intellectual center of contemplative intuitive understanding.

As Figure I shows, no different maps are presented for a lower and a higher instinctual center. Rather, the operation of ego-bound instinct, mapped by the three instinct enneagrams, stands in contrast with pure instinct which might be mapped by just three dots.

We may distinguish an instinctual, an emotional and a cognitive level of the personality; yet, since the instinctual realm is understood in this view as threefold, the personality or ego is said to comprise five centers .

Though, in the figure, instinct appears as belonging to both essence and personality, its functioning is different in either case. While in personality instinct is bound through the operation of the passions, in essence, or more exactly speaking, *in the essential mode*, instinct is free.

After having dwelt on personality as a whole and on a view of the fall into endarkenment and psychopathology, I now propose to zoom-in on the

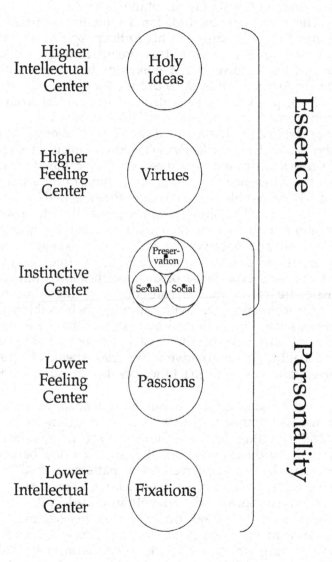

Figure I

subject, beginning with a guided tour of the egoic emotional center—the realm of the passions.

The word passion has, for a long time, carried a connotation of sickness. In his *Anthropologie* Kant says, "An emotion is like water that breaks through a dike, passion like a torrent that makes its bed deeper and deeper. An emotion is like a drunkenness that puts you to sleep; passion is like a disease that results from a faulty constitution or a poison." The idea became even more explicit in the early days of psychology. Thus Ribot, in his *Essai sur les Passions* writes: "Even if we can not regard all passions as diseases, they come so close, that the difference between them is almost ungraspable and it is impossible not to consider them related."

The word "passion" is appropriate for the lower emotions both in that they exist in interdependence with pain and because the individual is subjected to them as a passive agent lacking a free agent's characteristic experience of dis-identification from the passionate realm that is consequent to the intuition of transcendence. Notwithstanding their subjective presentation, these emotional states that we call passions are part of the "machine" or conditioned personality. Or, alternatively, we may speak of what drives and fuels the machine, besides an adulterated instinct.

Before saying more about the passions, however, let me say something about the enneagram—a geometric structure that became known in the west through Gurdjieff and which the esoteric school behind him and Ichazo conceived as a pattern embodying universal laws, discernable in all manner of processes.

More specifically, the triangle inscribed in its circle alludes to a universal threefoldness permeating all existence in the form of an "active," "passive," and a "neutralizing" force; while the points around it, with the exception of those in the 3 and 6 positions called "shock points," stand for a sevenfold pattern in natural cycles. The "Law of Three" is said to apply to the Divine Principle, the "Law of Seven" to Creation. The "invisible" shock points constitute a link between the realms of being and becoming, an influence from a higher level than that in which a given process unfolds.

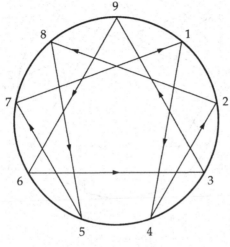

Figure II

The enneagram is a map through which the structure of each of the five personality realms, "centers," mentioned thus far may be represented: those of three instincts, that of the passions and that of the fixations.

Beyond personality, it is also the map and model for the two additional essence centers that, according to tradition, it is possible to develop through "intentional striving and conscious suffering."

Inspection of the enneagram of the passions in Figure III shows that three of them occupy a position more central than the others. Because of the symbolism of the enneagram—according to which the different points along it correspond to degrees and intervals in the musical scale—psychospiritual laziness, at the top, stands as the most basic of all, being, as it were, the Do of the passions.

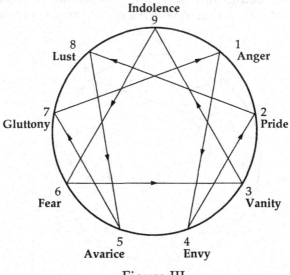

Figure III

While the proposition of a psychological inertia, laziness, echoes the learning theory of neurosis as conditioning, the other two points in the inner triangle summarize the Freudian theory of neurosis—as an expression of childhood anxiety—and the existential one—that envisions inauthentic being and "bad faith" as the basis of pathology.

The fact that these three mental states are mapped at the corners of the triangle in the enneagram of passions conveys a statement to the effect that these are cornerstones of the whole emotional edifice, and that the ones mapped between them can be explained as interactions in different proportions of the same. Anger, for instance, is a hybrid of psychological inertia with pretending, as is also pride, though with a pre-dominance of inertia or vanity respectively.

The interconnections shown between these three points, in the form of sides of the triangle, constitute psychodynamic connections, so that each may be said to underlie the next in a sequence mapped by arrows between them in a particular direction.

If we read this psychodynamic sequence starting at the top, we may say that a lack of the sense of being, implicit in the "robotization" of sloth, deprives the individual of a basis from which to act, and thus leads to fear. Since we must act in the world, however, much as we may fear it, we feel prompted to solve this contradiction by acting from a false self rather than courageously being who we are. We then build a mask between ourselves and the world, we identify with it, and vanity thus arises. To the extent that we identify with our mask, however, we forget who we truly are, we perpetuate the ontic obscuration that, in turn, supports fear, and so on, around the vicious circle.

Looking at the enneagram of the passions, the reader will not have failed to notice that seven of these are no different from the Gregorian capital sins (from *caput*, head). It may be observed that those not mentioned by the Christian tradition are precisely the cornerstones in the system, the shock-points, tradi-tionally said to be invisible.

I think that the present conception of the lower emotional center or, in other words, the enneagram of passions, provides a more comprehensive account of neurosis than we find in theories that have proposed a specific one of these attitudinal atmospheres to be the ultimate background of all psychopathology—regardless of neurotic style.

Just as Freud elaborated a fear-centered inter-pretation of life and human relations and the exis-tentialists have emphasized the need to be-for-others

and inauthenticity, Karen Horney has claimed, like
Christian writers, that pride is the crucial psychological
defect; Melanie Klein has underscored envy, and
Fairbairn and Guntrip have emphazised the schizoid
phenomenon related—as we shall see—with point 5.

Perhaps it is closer to the truth to say—as
Protoanalysis implies—that a particular one of these
interpretations will be more appropriate to the situation
or character structure of a given individual, even
though all points of view apply to each. Thus the
diagnosis of the ruling passion can constitute a *central*
interpretation, next in importance and transforming
potential, according to this view, only to the pointing
out of the cognitive ego or fixation, the main
representative of "Satan" within the psyche, in the
language of the vision transmitted by Ichazo.

Rather than characterizing the passions, which I
will be doing in the successive chapters of this book, I
will only say now that we need to attune ourselves to
an original meaning in the traditional words, seeing for
instance in "anger" a more inward and basic "standing
against" reality than explosive irritation; "lust" as more
than an inclination to sex or even pleasure: a passion
for excess or an excessive passionateness, to which
sexual satisfaction is only one possible source of
gratification; likewise "gluttony" will be here understood, not in its narrow sense of a passion for food, but
in the wider sense of a hedonistic bias and an insatiable
desire for more. "Avarice," too, may or may not include
money hoarding, and will designate a fearful and
greedy holding on of a more generalized nature—a
withdrawn alternative to the outreaching attachment of
lust, gluttony, envy and other emotions.

Just as the sides of the inner triangle indicate
psychodynamic connections between the mental states
mapped at points nine - six - three - nine in that
sequence, it remains to be said that the lines connecting

points 1 - 4 - 2 - 8 - 5 - 7 - 1 likewise indicate psychodynamic relations, so that each passion may be understood as grounded in the previous one, as the reader may explore in his own experience.

In contrast to the view of Christian theologians to the effect that there is a hierarchy of seriousness between the capital sins—and also in contrast to the view of contemporary psychology to the effect that the characters not only arise from different stages in development but also are more or less resistant to change and more or less pathological than others—the

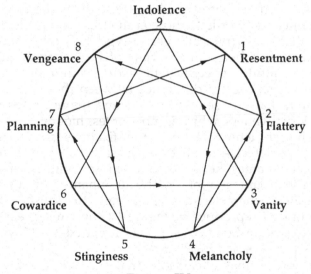

Figure IV

present view asserts that the passions are equivalent both in ethico-theological and in prognostic terms. This statement may be translated to imply that, while some characters may be more successfully treated than others by present day psychotherapy and its interpretation of mind, the path of transformation is not radically better or worse for the bearers of different personalities in terms of the traditional approaches of work on self and meditation.

Perhaps this may be better explained through a piece of conventional theology concerning sin. Since Saint Thomas the classic distinction differentiates in sin two aspects: the more visible one of harm to others or self, in view of which emotional factors such as envy or wrath constitute the basis of non-virtuous action; and another aspect common to all sins which is that of side-tracking the soul from the divine.

While some psychological types, at least consciously, suffer more (typically those at the bottom of the enneagram) or less (those at the top), and while it is true that some (typically ennea-type VIII) cause more suffering to others—in the view of Protoanalysis they only constitute an equivalent *spiritual* hindrance, and there is also a great difference between the degree of apparent harm to self and others and the *real* measure of destructiveness, which is more or less hidden.

Though Ichazo defined the fixations as specific cognitive defects—facets of a delusional system in the ego—the names he gave to them sometimes reflect either the same notion as the dominant passions or associated characteristics that fail to satisfy the definition. I reproduce in Figure IV the enneagram of fixations according to Ichazo as reported by Lilly in Tart's *Transpersonal Psychologies*.[3]

Here it may be seen that the reference to resentment in point I is nearly redundant with "anger," and in the case of point 2, flattery refers mostly to "self-flattery," which is inseparable from the self-aggrandizement of pride. In the case of point 3 Ichazo did provide words with significantly different meanings for the emotional and the cognitive aspects of a

---

[3] "The Arica Training" chapter by John C. Lilly and Joseph E. Hart in *Transpersonal Psychologies*, edited by Charles Tart (Psychological Processes, El Cerrito, 1983).

character, and yet I have taken the position of disagreeing with his ascription of restlessness in the pursuit of achievement to the fixation realm, and of deceit to that of the emotional realm of the passions.[4]

In the "Mendelejeffian" nomenclature proposed by Ichazo in Arica, using terms beginning with "ego" and containing the first letters of the fixation, the designation "ego-melan" does contain information different from envy, for it addresses itself to the "masochistic" aspect of the character in question, the seeking of love and care through the intensification of pain and helplessness. Yet in point 5, again, the word he proposes, "stinginess," fails to go beyond the scope of avarice. The same is the case in point 6, for cowardice does not give much more information than the passion of fear. Though cowardice does entail a meaning of "fear in the face of fear," I have preferred to regard accusation, especially self-accusation, as the central cognitive problem of ennea-type VI, as I elaborate in the corresponding chapter.

When I first heard Ichazo teach Protoanalysis at his lectures in the Instituto de Psicologia Aplicada, the word he used for the fixation in point 7 was *charlataneria*, Spanish for charlatanism. Later, addressing himself to an English-speaking audience he labeled the personality "ego-plan." Planning evokes the tendency of ennea-type VII to live on projects and fantasies and to substitute imagination for action.

In speaking of "ego-venge," again Ichazo points to a characterological disposition that may be regarded central in the corresponding ennea-type, and provides information complementary to that of its "lusty" aspect: ennea-type VIII is not only dionysian and passionate,

---

[4] In Chapter 3, I propose the appropriateness of regarding vanity as belonging to the same sphere of pride (a passion for being in the eyes of the other rather than a passion for self-inflation) and for regarding deceit and self-deception as the cognitive aspect of ennea-type III (in virtue of which the individual identifies with the false self).

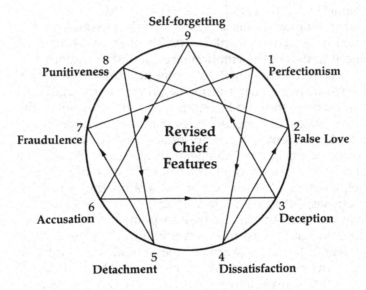

Figure V

but hard and dominant, the bearer of a prejudiced view of life as struggle where the powerful succeed.

In the case of point 9, once more Ichazo's word "ego-in," in reference to indolence, is redundant with "laziness," the word used for the dominant passion. If laziness is understood as psychospiritual inertia—akin to an automatization of life and a loss of inwardness —the implicit conviction underlying the life strategy of ennea-type IX may be regarded as one that over-emphasizes the value of over-adaptation and abnegation.

A slightly different emphasis comes into play if we choose names for the fixations in view of the identification claimed by Ichazo between these and the "chief feature" of each personality type. The words in Figure V fit both definitions of "fixation": they are appropriate to designate the most outstanding feature in the corresponding character structure and they may be understood as inseparable from a cognitive operation.

Thus deception (more appropriate than "deceit" in this context) involves self-deception as well as pretending to others, and a cognitive confusion between what is the case and what is claimed to be true. In the case of vindictiveness, too, there is reference to the chief characteristic of punitiveness in ennea-type VIII, and also to an implicit view—inseparable from it—that irrationally seeks to make right the past through a retribution of damage or hurt in the present.

In the case of the false generosity and satisfaction of ennea-type II, again this may be regarded as the chief feature and a cognitive mistake on the part of the person akin to deception. The same may be said of the the self-frustrating characteristic of ennea-type IV, which involves looking at what is lacking rather than perceiving what is there, and for the detachment of ennea-type V, inseparable from a view to the effect that it is better to "go it alone."

Early in the life of my first group in Berkeley, a student, Dr. Larry Effron, summarized the characters using caricatures which he presented to me on the occasion of a birthday party.

In those caricatures one could see ennea-type I not as one boiling in resentment, but as a mountain climber animated by a disposition of "trying harder." I have usually called him the "perfectionist," even though this is a word with which others, particularly ennea-type III, can easily identify as well. While in ennea-type III there is a formal perfectionism, here it is a moral perfectionism that is characteristic.

Ennea-type II is seen in this composition in its histrionic and flamboyant aspect not necessarily suggested by the words pride or flattery. As we shall see, traditional hysterical personality falls in here. Ennea-type III as involving self-deception as to who one is and over-identification with the social role, is represented as an erectly standing, neat and successful professional. In contrast with this winner, however, the collage shows in point IV the picture of one ill-treated by life, a crucified suffering victim.

Point 5 is appropriately the caricature of isolation which disposition may be regarded as the interpersonal style that emerges from and sustains retentiveness. The warrior in point 6 again conveys a connotation apparently very different from fear, and yet alludes to a characteristic tendency of ennea-type VI to be at war with self and others—as well as a dutiful pursuit of heroism, arisen from fear of authority and sustained through a counterphobic avoidance of the experience of fear. The warrior image is not an appropriate caricature of all ennea-type VI individuals, however. The figure in point 7 has, instead of a head, what seems to be wiring. It suggests an insubstantial head that contains plans, abstractive books and artifacts.

At point 8 we see somebody who stands on a platform in order to talk down to people, to harangue them with powerful voice and demeanor. It is appropriate, though it leaves out a representation of sadistic behavior.

At point 9 the human figure is sitting as fits a depiction of laziness, and the whole drawing suggests vacationing under the shade of a palm tree on a tropical beach. While appropriate to the depiction of the passion for laziness in the conventional sense, it does not allude to the psychological laziness of one who does not want to look at himself, nor to the characteristic of resigned over-adaptation of ennea-type IX.

Rather than illustrating the characters with the above described caricatures, the essence of which can be translated into words, I have shown in Figure VI—as additional information—a drawing by Margarita

Figure VI

Fernandez that conveys some of the constitutional and gestural characteristics of the ennea-types.

The survey of the fixations thus far, while providing characterological information, has done little to explicate these psychological processes as specifically cognitive defects. We may say that the exposure of any of the interpersonal styles into which the passions, according to this theory, crystallize, involves a measure of idealization; a hidden view to the effect that such is the way to live. In the psychotherapeutic process sometimes it is possible to recover the memory of a time in life when a decision was made to take revenge, never to love again, to go it alone and never to trust, and so on. When this is possible we can still make explicit many computations that a person has been taking as truths ever since and which can be questioned; computations of a child in pain and panic that need to be revised, as Ellis proposes in his *Rational-Emotive Therapy.*

However true it may be that every interpersonal style involves a cognitive bias, in the sense of an implicit assumption that such is the best way to be, it is my impression that this cognitive bias does not exhaust an analysis of the intellectual aspect of each personality orientation, and thus—as I have announced in the Foreword—I am examining throughout this book for each character the metaphysical mistakes or illusions (confusions about Being) that perpetuate ego identification. Thus it is that I elaborate on what in the Foreword I have called the Nasruddin Theory of Neurosis: a view to the effect that a loss of being or ontic obscuration[5] underlies each of the passions and these, in turn, are perpetuated by a search for being in the wrong place.

Through the systematic analysis of all character structures in light of ontic obscuration, I think I have fulfilled an ambition formulated by Guntrip, who in *Schizoid Phenomena Object Relations and the Self* writes, "Psychoanalytic theory had for a long time the appearance of the exploration of a circle which had no obvious center until ego psychology got on the way. Exploration had to begin with peripheral phenomena— behavior, moods, symptoms, conflicts, 'mental mechanisms,' erotic drives, aggression, fears, guilt, psychotic and psychoneurotic states, instincts and impulses, erotogenic zones, maturational stages and so on. All

---

[5] I prefer to use this expression instead of "ontic insecurity" proposed by R.D. Laing for the same meaning, for "ontic insecurity" evokes a quality that "ontic obscuration" entails in the specific instance of the "fear family" of characters (V, VI and VII).

these are naturally important and must find their place in the total theory, but actually it is all secondary to some absolutely fundamental factor which is the 'core' of the 'person as such.' " Such a fundamental factor at the root of all passions (deficiency motivation) is a thirst for being that exists side by side with a dim apprehension of being-loss.

I will only add to this theory at this point the contention that wherever "being" may seem to be, it is not; and that being can only be found in the most unlikely place, or rather in the most unlikely manner: through the acceptance of non-being and a journey through emptiness.

Chapter One

ANGRY VIRTUE

(Ennea-type I)

1. Anger and Perfectionism

"We may consider wrath in three ways," says Saint Thomas in *Questiones Disputatae*: "Firstly, a wrath which resides in the heart (*Ira Cordis*); also, inasmuch as it flows into words (*Ira Locutionis*), and thirdly, in that it becomes actions (*Ira Actiones*)." The survey scarcely brings to mind the characteristics of the perfectionistic type as we will be portraying it here. Yes, there is anger in the heart, mostly in the form of resentment, yet not so prominently as anger may be experienced by the lusty, the envious or the cowardly. As for verbal behavior, it is most characteristic of the anger type to be *controlled* in the expression of anger, in any of its explicit forms: we are in the presence of a well-behaved, civilized type, not a spontaneous one. In regard to action, ennea-type I individuals do express anger, yet mostly unconsciously, not only to themselves but to others, for they do so in a way that is typically rationalized; in fact, much of this personality may be understood as a reaction formation against anger: a denial of destructiveness through a deliberate, well-intentioned attitude.

Oscar Ichazo's definition of anger as a "standing against reality" has the merit of addressing a more basic

issue than the feeling or expression of emotion. Still, it
may be useful to point out at the outset that the label
"anger type" is scarcely evocative of the typical
psychological characteristics of the personality style in
question—which is critical and demanding rather than
consciously hateful or rude. Ichazo called the ennea-
type "ego-resent," which seems a psychologically more
exact portrayal of the emotional disposition involved:
one of protest and assertive claims rather than mere
irritability. In my own teaching experience, I started out
calling the character's fixation "intentional goodness";
later I shifted to labelling it "perfectionism." This seems
appropriate to designate a rejection of what is in terms
of what is felt and believed should be.

Christian writers who shared an awareness of anger
as a capital sin, that is to say, of anger as one of the basic
psychological obstacles to true virtue, mostly seem to
have failed to realize that it is precisely under the guise
of virtue that unconscious anger finds its most
characteristic form of expression. An exception is St.
John of the Cross, who in his *Dark Night of the Soul*
writes with characterological exactitude as he describes
the sin of wrath in spiritual beginners:

"There are other of these spiritual persons, again,
who fall into another kind of spiritual wrath: this
happens when they become irritated at the sins of
others, and keep watch on those others with a sort of
uneasy zeal. At times the impulse comes to them to
reprove them angrily, and occasionally they go so far as
to indulge it and set themselves up as masters of virtue.
All this is contrary to spiritual meekness." And he adds:
"There are others who are vexed with themselves when
they observe their own imperfection, and display an
impatience that is not humility; so impatient are they
about this that they would fain be saints in a day. Many
of these persons purport to accomplish a great deal and
make grand resolutions; yet, as they are not humble
and have no misgivings about themselves, the more

resolutions they make, the greater is the fall and the greater their annoyance, since they have not the patience to wait for that which God will give them when it pleases Him."[1]

2. Trait Structure

In what follows, I have undertaken to show something of the structure of the perfectionistic character in terms of the underlying traits that may be discerned through a conceptual analysis of some hundred and seventy descriptors.

Anger

More than a trait among others, "anger" may be regarded as the generalized emotional background and original root of this character structure. The more specific manifestation of the emotional experience of anger is resentment, and this is most commonly felt in connection with a sense of injustice in face of the responsibilities and efforts the individual undertakes in larger measure than others. It is inseparable from the criticism of others (or significant others) for displaying less zeal, and sometimes it involves the adoption of a martyr role. The most visible expression of anger occurs when it is perceived as justified, and can in such cases take the form of vehement "righteous indignation."

In addition, anger is present in the form of irritation, reproach and hatefulness that remain largely unexpressed, since perceived destructiveness conflicts with the virtuous self-image characteristic of the ennea-type. Beyond the perception of anger at an emotional level, however, we may say that the passion of anger permeates the whole of ennea-type I character and is

[1] *The Dark Night of the Soul*, translated by E. Allison Peers (New York: Doubleday and Co., 1959), p.53.

the dynamic root of drives or attitudes such as we discuss in connection with the remaining clusters: criticality, demandingness, dominance and assertiveness, perfectionism, over-control, self-criticism and discipline.

Criticality

If conscious and manifest anger is not always one of the most striking characteristics of this personality, the more common traits in the ennea-type may be understood as derivatives of anger, expressions of unconscious anger or anger equivalents. One of these is criticality, which is not only manifest in explicit fault finding, but sometimes creates a subtle atmosphere that causes others to feel awkward or guilty. Criticality may be described as intellectual anger more or less unconscious of its motive. I say this because, even though it is possible that criticism occurs in the context of felt anger, the most salient quality of this criticality is a sense of constructive intent, a desire to make others or oneself better. Through intellectual criticism, thus, anger is not only expressed but justified and rationalized—and, through this, denied. Moral reproaches are another form of perfectionistic disapproval and not just expressions of anger, but a form of manipulation in the service of unacknowledged demandingness—whereby "I want" is transformed into "You should." Accusation thus entails the hope of affecting somebody's behavior in the direction of one's wishes.

A specific form of criticality in ennea-type I is that bound to ethnocentrism and other forms of prejudice, in which case there is vilification, invalidation and the wish to "reform" inquisitorially those who constitute an outgroup to one's race, nation, class, church, and so on.

Demandingness

Demandingness also can be understood as an expression of anger: a vindictive over-assertiveness in regard to one's wishes in response to early frustration. Along with demandingness proper, we may group together characteristics such as those which make these individuals the most disciplinarian both in the sense of inhibiting spontaneity and the pursuit of pleasure in others, as well as exacting hard work and excellent performance. They tend to sermonize, preach and teach without regard for the appropriateness of such a role—even though this compulsive characteristic of theirs may find its niche in activities such as those of school teacher and preacher.

Together with this corrective orientation is that of being controlling, and this not only in relation to people but to environments or personal appearance: an obsessive is likely to prefer a highly "manicured" garden, for instance, where plants are in clear order and trees pruned into artificial shape, over one that conveys a "Taoistic" organic complexity.

Dominance

Though already implicit in intellectual criticism, which would be without force if not in a context of moral or intellectual authority, and implicit also in the controlling-demanding-disciplinarian characteristic (for how would that be effective without authority), it seems appropriate to regard dominance as a relatively independent trait, comprising such descriptors as an autocratic style, a self-confident and dignified assertiveness, an aristocratic self-concept and a superior, haughty, disdainful and perhaps condescending and patronizing demeanor.

Dominance, too, may be regarded as an implicit expression or a transformation of anger, yet this orientation towards a position of power entails subordinate strategies as the above and also a sense of entitlement, on the basis of high standards, diligence, cultural and family background, intelligence, and so on.

Perfectionism

Most characteristically, however, the pursuit of mastery in the anger type implies the endorsement of the moral system or human hierarchy in which authority is vested. It may be said that the perfectionist is more obedient to the abstract authority of norms or office than the concrete authority of persons. Also as Millon remarks, "people with obsessive personality not only do adhere to societal rules and customs, but vigorously espouse and defend them." Such vehement interest in principles, morals and ideals is not only an expression of submission to the demands of a strong superego, but, interpersonally, an instrument of manipulation and dominance, for these enthusiastically endorsed norms are imposed on others and, as was commented above, serve as a cover for personal wishes and demands. Yet ennea-type I individuals are not only oriented to "Law and Order," and themselves obedient to norms, they also subordinate themselves to people in the position of unquestionable authority.

The emphatic endorsement of norms and sanctioned authority usually implies a conservative orientation or, to adopt David Riesman's language, the tendency to be "tradition directed," (a trait shared with ennea-type IX). It is hard to separate, except conceptually, two aspects of perfectionism: the cathexis of ideal standards, i.e., the vehement endorsement of norms, and the "perfectionistic intention," i.e., a striving to be better. Both kinds of "good intention" support a sense of personal goodness, kindness and disinterestedness, and distract the individual from the preconscious perception of self as angry, evil and selfish. (Among the descriptors grouped in the cluster are included "good

boy/girl," "goody-goody," "honest," "fair," "formal,"
"moral," and so on.)

Not only is compulsive virtue a derivative of anger
through the operation of reaction formation, it is also
the expression of anger turned inwards, for it amounts
to becoming one's own harsh critic, policeman and
disciplinarian. Also, we may conceive a group of traits,
ranging from orderliness and cleanliness to a puritanical disposition, as a means to evoke affection
through merit and a response to an early emotional
frustration.

Particularly important for the therapeutic process is
the understanding of how perfectionism serves anger
by preventing its acknowledgement. More specifically,
it serves (by supporting felt entitlement) the unconscious expression of anger as dominance, criticality and
demandingness. The image of the crusader may serve
as a paradigm for this situation: one who is entitled to
break skulls in virtue of the excellence of his cause and
his noble aspirations. When the strategy maneuver is
visible enough, we find it appropriate to speak not only
of "compulsive" virtue but of "hypocritical" virtue—for
even though (as Horney points out) a certain level of
honesty is characteristic of the perfectionist, his
obsessive preoccupation with right and wrong, or good
and bad, entails an unconscious dishonesty in its intent.

From the preceding analysis it is clear that the
psychodynamic relation between anger and perfectionism is reciprocal: just as we may surmise that the
strategy of striving to do better has been preceded by
anger in the course of early development and continues
to be fueled by unconscious anger, it is easy to
understand how anger itself continually arises from
self-frustration and from interpersonal consequences of
the irritating activity and rigidity of the perfectionist.

While I have grouped together under the single
label of "perfectionism" those traits ranging from "love
of order," "law abidingness," and "an orientation to

rules," to "do-goodism" and "dutiful nurturance," such as make people adopt fathering or mothering roles toward others, I have grouped the three traits of "over-control," "self-criticism" and "discipline" separately below. These traits stand in the same relationship to perfectionism as "criticality," "demandingness" and "dominance" stand in relation to perfectionistic anger directed toward others. Just as criticality, demandingness and dominance are hard to separate, over-control, self-criticism and discipline—three attitudes toward oneself that constitute, we may say, the underside of perfectionism—are closely related as facets of a single underlying disposition. Perfectionism may be singled out, along with anger, as a pervasive dynamic factor in the character and as its root strategy.

Over-control

What dominance—a transformation of anger—is to others, self-control is to perfectionism. Excessive control over one's behavior goes hand-in-hand with a characteristic rigidity, a sense of awkwardness, a lack of spontaneity with the consequent difficulty to function in non-structured situations and whenever improvisation is required. To others, the over-control may result in boringness. Excessive control over one's self extends, beyond outer behavior to psychological functioning in general, so that thinking becomes excessively rule bound, i.e. logical and methodical, with loss of creativity and leaps of intuition. Control over feeling, on the other hand, leads not only to the blocking of emotional expression but even to alienation from emotional experience.

Self-Criticism

What the criticism of others is to anger, self-criticism is to perfectionism. Though self-disparagement may not be apparent to the outside observer and tends to be hidden behind a virtuous and self-dignified image, the inability to accept oneself and the process of self-vilification not only are the source of chronic emotional frustration (and unconscious anger) but an ever present psychodynamic background for the perfectionistic need to try harder in the pursuit of worthiness.

Discipline

What angry demandingness is to anger, an implicitly hateful and exploitative demanding from oneself is to perfectionism. Beyond do-goodism proper, i.e., an orientation toward correction and moral ideas, self-demanding involves a willingness to strive at the expense of pleasure, which makes ennea-type I individuals hard-working and disciplined as well as over-serious. And just as a vindictive element may be discerned in interpersonal demands, a masochistic element may be discerned in the postponement of pleasure and natural impulses, for beyond a mere subordination of pleasure to duty the individual develops, to a greater or lesser extent, a "puritanical" disposition of being opposed to pleasure and the play of instinct.

3. Existential Psychodynamics

Before considering the existential psychodynamics of ennea-type I, it may be well to reiterate the postulate that is to be articulated through the contemplation of the nine characters in the book: that passions arise out of a background of ontic obscuration; that the loss of a sense of I-am-ness sustains a craving-for-being that is manifested in the differentiated form of the ego's nine basic emotions.

In the case of ennea-type I, the proximity of the character to that of psychospiritual laziness (indeed the fact of being a hybrid between it and pride) makes the issue of ontic obscuration something that lies near the

E.J. Gold, *The View From Above,*
pen and ink, 5 3/4" x 11".

foreground of their psychological style. This is to say that there is in the life-attitude of ennea-type I a loss of the sense of being which, as is the case in the three characters at the upper region of the enneagram, manifests as an "unconsciousness of unconsciousness"[2] that gives them a particular self-satisfaction, opposite to felt deficiency or to "poverty in spirit" of those at the bottom of the enneagram. Unconscious dissatisfaction, however, is converted into the hottest of the passions, which, however ignored by active unconsciousness, underlies the quality of interpersonal relationships.

While ontic obscuration involves a sort of psychological coarsening in the case of ennea-type VIII and ennea-type IX psychology as will be seen, in ennea-type I this tendency is covered up by an excessive refinement; it could be said that reactive formation also takes place at the ontic level: perceived ontic deficiency becomes stimulus for compensation through activities purporting to sustain false abundance. The main activity that promises abundance to the ennea-type I mind is the enactment of perfection. We might say that precisely in virtue of this obscuration, the search for being can turn into a search for the substitute being of the good life, in which behavior fits an extrinsic criterion of value. The wrathful are in special need, however, of understanding Lao-Tse's statement:

"Virtue (Te) does not seek to be virtuous;
precisely because of this it is virtue."

In other words: Virtue, by not being "virtuous," is virtue.

It would be too narrow however, to say that the substitute for being in ennea-type I is virtue, for sometimes the quality of life is not so much a moralistic one but one with the quality of "correction," a goodness of

[2]See Chapter 9.

fit between behavior and a world of principles; or a goodness of fit between ongoing life and some implicit or explicit code.

On the whole, it may be said that the preconscious perception of being-scarcity and the imagination of destructiveness and evil in ennea-type I is compensated for with an impulse to being a "person of character": one endowed with a certain over-stability, a certain strength to resist temptations and stand by what is right. Also, loss of being and value supports activity designed to sustain the impression of somebody worthy which, as we have seen, is sought through a sort of worship of goodness and worthiness.

In the Nasruddin corpus of jokes, ennea-type I may be recognized in the grammarian whom Nasruddin, as boatman, carries to "the other shore." After Nasruddin answers some inquiry from the grammarian with incorrect speech, the grammarian asks, "Haven't you studied grammar?" At Nasruddin's answering to the effect that this was not the case, he proffers out of righteous and well informed self-satisfaction, "You have lost half of your life." Later, Nasruddin asks the grammarian, "Do you know how to swim?" And since our worthy grammarian responds that this is not the case, Nasruddin remarks, "Then you have lost your *whole* life, for we're sinking."

The joke poignantly alludes to the dissociation between the "grammarian mentality" and life. A process of rigidification and loss of meaning through excessive concern for form and detail has taken place. Even when in the pursuit of goodness rather than that of formal correction, such as in school matters, there is beyond consciously cultivated kindness a coldness that entails both lovelessness and insubstantiality, or being-loss.

Chapter Two

EGOCENTRIC GENEROSITY

(Ennea-type II)

1. Pride and Histrionism

In Christianity pride is not only regarded as one of the capital sins, but the first and most serious one—more fundamental than the others. In that great monument of the Christian vision, Dante's *Divine Comedy*, we find Lucifer—whose pride prompted him to say "I" in the presence of the Only One—at the center of hell itself shaped as a cone sloping to the center of the earth. This enormous cavity, according to Dante's myth, was created by the weight of the prideful angel upon his fall from heaven. On Mount Purgatory, where the pilgrims escalate successive terraces in the traditional sequence of the sins, the cornice of pride is the lowest, nearest to the mountain's foundation.

Dante's near-contemporary Chaucer in *The Canterbury Tales*[1] gives us a good but incomplete characterological allusion to proud people in "The Parson's Tale," which is essentially a preaching on the sins. He mentions among the "evil branches that spring from pride": disobedience, boasting, hypocrisy, scorn, arrogance, impudence, swelling of the heart, insolence,

[1] *The Canterbury Tales,* modern English version by J. U. Nicholson (New York: Garden City Books, 1934).

elation, impatience, contumacy, presumption, irreverence, obstinacy and vainglory. The picture that these traits add to characterizes an individual who not only asserts his own value, but does so with an aggressive self-elevation vis-a-vis others and a disregard for established values and authorities.

True to life as Chaucer's portrayal may be, it fails to convey the whole range of the manifestations of pride-centered character. Fundamental to it is the strategy of *giving* in the service of both seduction and self-elevation. The "official psychology" of ennea-type II has failed to properly describe this characteristic false generosity in the character, for the descriptions of hysterical character have emphasized impulsive egocentricity, whereas it would be more exact to speak of a complementarity of egocentricity and seeming generosity. The account of hysterical character also tends to interpret the eroticism of hysterical personality as a phenomenon of ultimate sexual origin, whereas it may be truer to regard eroticism as a means of seductiveness inspired by a love wish.

The view of pride as more sinful than other inclinations may be a good teaching strategy to counteract proud people's lightness about their way of being, yet this is not the view of the body of psychological knowledge that I am presenting in these pages. According to Protoanalysis, all the passions are of an equivalent seriousness, and though one is regarded as more fundamental—accidia or psychological deadening—this is not a statement concerning degrees of sinfulness or a ranking according to prognosis. The position of point 9 in the middle of the enneagram, rather, evokes the fact that laziness may be regarded as a neutral middle point of the spectrum of the passions and that active unconsciousness, though present in every fallen mind, is in the foreground of the ennea-type IX phenomenon.

We may envision pride as a passion for self-inflation: or, in other words, a passion for the aggrandizement of the self image.

The corresponding fixation or fixed and implicit preconception involved in pride, Ichazo successively called "flattery" and "ego-flat"—not only in reference to flattery towards others, but to the self-flattery implicit in self-aggrandizement. The word has the disadvantage of evoking a person whose behavior is mostly that of flattery—whereas the reality is that of a personality given not only to flattery but, in similar measure, to disdain. The person flatters those who through nearness gratify his pride, disdains most of the rest in haughty superiority. More than anybody else, the proud practice something that Idries Shah has called M.C.O.—"mutual comfort operation."[2]

From its position in the enneagram, we see that pride stands in the "hysteroid" corner of it, aligned with the preoccupation with self-image that is the essence of vanity. In all three character types mapped at this corner—II, III and IV—we may say that there operates a mistaken sense of "being" in what others see and value, so that it is the self-image rather than the true self upon which the psyche gravitates, out of which action flows and on which is supported a person's sense of value.

Points 2 and 4 stand in opposite positions in regard to point 3, and involve internal gestures of expansion and contraction of the self-image, respectively. Whereas envy tends to sadness, pride characteristically is supported by a happy internal atmosphere; ennea-type IV is "tragic," ennea-type II "comic."

Just as with other sets of antipodal characters in the enneagram there is an affinity between those at points 7 and 2. Both the gluttons and the proud are gentle, sweet and warm people; both may be said to be seductive; and they are both narcissistic in the general sense of being delighted with themselves. Also, both are

[2] Idries Shah, *Reflections* (Zenith Books, London, 1968).

impulsive; moreover, they use seductiveness in the service of their impulsiveness, yet they do this in different ways: the proud seduces emotionally and the glutton intellectually. The main contrast between the two characters is that, while the glutton is amiable and diplomatic, the proud can be either sweet or aggressive (so that, as I have sometimes remarked, their motto might be "make love *and* war"). Their narcissism also differs. We may say that the former is sustained through an intellectual apparatus: the activity of charlatanism in the broad sense of the word. In ennea-type II it is supported by a more naive falling in love with oneself, an emotional process of self-loving through identification with the glorified self-image and repression of the deprecated image. Also, the narcissism of the glutton is more inner-directed, in that he becomes an arbiter of his own values, as Samuel Butler has stated in describing one of his characters as "a messenger from his church to himself."[3] Ennea-type II is more outer-directed, so that there is more admixture of borrowed values in the glorified self-image.

A polarity also exists between ennea-types II and VIII, pride and lust, in that both are impulsive and also arrogant—though ennea-type II adopts more often an attitude of being so good as not to need to compete, whereas the lusty is intensely competitive and visibly arrogant. The characterological constellation of ennea-type II is acknowledged in current psychology under the labels of "hysterical" or "histrionic" personality, yet I am not aware of any discussion of pride as a major aspect of its dynamics.

[3] Samuel Butler, *The Characters* (Cleveland: Case Western University, 1970).

2. Trait Structure

Pride

While a number of descriptors might be grouped together as direct manifestations of pride—i.e., the imaginary exaltation of self-worth and attractiveness, "playing the part of the princess," demanding privileges, boasting, needing to be the center of attention, and so on—there are others which may be understood as psychological corollaries of pride, and to them I now turn.

Love Need

The intense love need of ennea-type II individuals may be sometimes obscured by their characteristic independence—particularly when in the presence of frustration and humiliated pride. The proud person can rarely be fulfilled in life without a great love. The excessively romantic orientation of ennea-type II toward life can be understood as the result of an early love frustration associated with a loss of support in one's experience of personal value. Just as the need to confirm an inflated sense of worth overflows into an erotic motivation, pride overflows in the need for love (in turn expressed through physical and emotional intimacy), for the need to regard oneself as special is satisfied through the love of another. The need for intimacy of ennea-type II makes of the person a "touchy-feely" type and at a subtler level leads to an intolerance of limits and to invasiveness. Also, the strong need for love of the proud makes them "over-involved" in relationships and possessive. Theirs is a possessiveness supported in such seductiveness as has inspired the expression "femme fatale" (which suggests that seductiveness serves a destructive power drive).

Hedonism

Hedonism may also be understood as a trait related to the need for love, in that the wish for pleasure can be usually seen as a substitute for pleasure. Indeed these persons typically need to be loved erotically or through delicate expression of tenderness in the measure to which they equate being loved with being pleased, like the princess in Grimm's fairy tale of "The Princess and the Pea," whose noble blood is discovered in the fact that she is distressed by a pea under the mattress. The affectionate and tender ennea-type II individual can become a fury when not indulged and made to feel loved through pampering such as is characteristic of a spoiled child.

The compulsive pursuit of pleasure of the ennea-type II person naturally supports the gay persona of histrionic people, with its pretended contentedness and animation. It is reflected, also, through a propensity to be frustrated and when not specially pleased (through attention, novelty, stimulation), through a low tolerance to routine, discipline and other obstacles to an irresponsible, playful life.

Seductiveness

It is understandable that the histrionic individual, bent on the pursuit of love and pleasure, is also keenly interested in being attractive. Such persons *work* for it, we might say, and are, above all, seductive. There are traits that we can, in turn, understand as tools of seductiveness—whether erotic or social. Thus the histrionic person is affectionate. Those who are in need of affection, because of being secretly insecure in regard to it, are, in turn, warm, supportive, sensitive, empathic... even though their display of love may have inspired epithets such as "superficial," "fickle," "unstable," and so forth. The support seductively offered by the individual is typically what may be called "emotional" support or perhaps "moral" support in the sense that one is an unconditional friend, yet may be not as helpful a person as may be suggested through the expression of feelings. (Ennea-type III and others can be more helpful when it comes to doing something practical.) Thus their seductiveness entails not only a histrionic love display but a failure to deliver, and motivationally speaking, a "giving to get" kind of generosity.

Flattery, too, may be valued as a means of seduction exhibited by ennea-type II individuals. It must be pointed out that ennea-type II only flatters those seen as worthy enough to be seduced.

Eroticism is thus one of the vehicles of seductiveness. If we look at the erotic inclination of the histrionic individual as something that serves a broader purpose of proving personal significance (rather than in biologistic Freudian terms), we can, I think, understand both eroticism and pride better.

Assertiveness

Along with an intense love need and its derivatives we may say that dominance is also a characteristic of ennea-type II and constitutes a derivative of pride. Rather than the harsh, tyrannical demandingness of ennea-type VIII and the moralistic dominance of ennea-type I, who exacts his due as an authority, ennea-type II gets his or her wishes met through daring assertiveness—*chutzpah*. It is the assertiveness of one who at the same time is supported in a good self-concept and propelled by a strong, uninhibited drive—which contributes to the aura of vitality of this adventurous character. (As I have remarked already, proud character involves a rare combination of tenderness and pugnacity.)

Another descriptor belonging to this category of assertiveness is that of willfulness, a trait of "having to have one's own way" even at the expense of an emotional "scene" or broken dishes.

Nurturance and False Abundance

Of great significance to the structure of proud character is the repression of neediness that pride involves. Much as we may be dealing with a zestful individual, who seems to be compulsively pursuing excitement and high drama, the person is typically unaware of and too proud to show the neediness that underlies her compulsion to please and to be extraordinary.

The proud are supposedly OK and very much better than OK, and to sustain this they must indeed pursue their pleasure in a compensatory manner. Yet nothing would be less OK than to be in need of love—for pride in the course of personality development has been particularly attached to an image of self as a giver rather than as a receiver: one filled with satisfaction to the point of generous overflowing.

Repression of neediness is not only supported by hedonism, but by vicarious identification with the neediness of others, of those towards whom the individual extends sympathy, empathy and seductive nurturance. Thus we may understand the frequent attraction of ennea-type II to children: they not only represent an unconstrained wildness, but little ones in need of protection. They sustain the proud in the sense of having much love to offer, as well as covertly satisfying their love need.

Histrionism

I could have written at the head of this trait cluster "histrionic implementation of the idealized self-image," in reference to what may be abstracted as an overriding strategy in ennea-type II of which false love and false self-satisfaction are a strong form of expression. The affectionate characteristic, however, can be seen as only one of the facets of the typical ideal image the proud enacts and identifies with.

Such image also contains the *happy* characteristic that we have already encountered in the analysis of seductiveness, an independence that involves the denial of dependency needs, and also a characteristic for which the word "free" might be an approximate term, if we understand it to be not the true freedom of liberation from characterological structures, but the freedom of willfulness, impulsiveness and wildness. This freedom is an ideal of impulse gratification that exists not only in the service of hedonism, but also as an avoidance of the humiliation of having to submit to somebody else's power, societal rules and all manner of constraints. Ennea-type II is not only too proud to conform to such rules, but is rebellious to authority in general—often in a mischievous and humorous way.

Also "intensity," which can be considered, along with wit, a means of attracting attention (and which feeds on the pursuit of pleasure), can be understood as an ingredient in a larger than life self-image. It is not only an addiction but also a form of posing and sustaining the illusion of positivity. The histrionic posing of ennea-type II is in contrast to the efforts of ennea-type III to implement the idealized self through achievement and performance—just as her histrionic manipulation (through scandalous expression of emotion) is in contrast with ennea-type III's explosiveness, which supervenes upon the breakdown of over-control.

Impressionable Emotionality

While ennea-types IV and II are distinctly the most emotional in the enneagram, ennea-type II can be regarded a more specifically emotional ennea-type, in that ennea-type IV emotionality frequently coexists with intellectual interest, while ennea-type II is not only a feeling type, but frequently an anti-intellectual one.

3. Existential Psychodynamics

If we understand pride as the result of an early love frustration that was equated in the child's mind with worthlessness (so that the impulse to worthiness and toward being special amounts to a compulsive repetition of the original maneuver of compensating for that early lack), it may be a mistake to continue to interpret pride as the elaboration of a love need. This may amount to putting the cart before the horse, since the intense love need of ennea-type II individuals is rather a consequence of pride than a more deeply seated antecedent. In line with the manner of interpretation undertaken thus far, which seeks to replace libido theory in the understanding of neurotic wants with an existential one, we can look at pride (as each of the passions) as a compensation for a perceived lack of value which goes hand-in-hand with an obscuration of the sense of one's being—the natural, original and truest support for one's sense of personal value.

We may say that, despite superficial elation, vitality and flamboyance, there lurks in proud character a secret recognition of emptiness—a recognition transformed into the pain of hysterical symptoms, into eroticism and clinging to love relationships. Notwithstanding the usual interpretation of this pain as a love pain, it may be more exact to regard it as no different from the universal pain of fallen consciousness, beyond type-bound characteristics. If we do so, we can understand that it may be transformed not only in libido, but that, interpreted as a sense of personal insignificance, it sustains the will to significance that is in the nature of pride.

E.J. Gold, *Me, Myself & I,*
pen and ink, 11" x 15", 1987.

Such an interpretation is useful, for it orients us to look for what in the present life of the individual is perpetuating this "hole" at the center of the personality. How this hole arises is not difficult to understand, for, as Horney has remarked, embracing the pursuit of glory amounts to something like selling one's soul to the devil—inasmuch as one's energy becomes involved in the realization of an image rather than in the realization of one's self.

The sense of being rests in the integrated wholeness of one's experience, and is not compatible with the repression of one's neediness any more than it is compatible with the failure to live one's true life (while occupied in dramatizing an ideal image for a selected audience of supporters). Excitement may capture one's attention and serves as an ontic pacifier from moment to moment, but only in a superficial level of awareness. The same may be said of pleasure. The individual fails to be as he or she is while driven to seek pleasure and excitement instead, and would like to live in the continuous ecstasy of being the center of attention.

False abundance, thus, is doomed to be, after all, an emotional lie that the individual does not fully believe—for otherwise he or she would not continue to be driven to fill up frantically the hole of deeply felt beinglessness. If it is ontic deficiency that supports pride and, indirectly, the whole edifice of pride-centered character, ontic deficiency is, in turn, brought about by each one of the traits that constitutes its structure: a gaiety that implies (by repression of sadness) a loss of reality; a hedonism that, in its chasing after immediate gratification, only affords a substitute satisfaction and not what growth requires; the compulsive indiscipline that goes along with this hedonism, with its free and wild characteristics of "hysteria," which also get in the way of accomplishing such life goals as would bring along a deeper satisfaction, and so on.

In conclusion, in recognition of this vicious circle whereby ontic insufficiency supports pride, which through its manifestation, in turn, supports ontic insufficiency, lies therapeutic hope; for the aim of therapy should not stop at providing the good relationship that was absent in early life: it can include re-educating the individual toward self-realization and the daily elaboration of that deep satisfaction that comes from an authentic existence.

Chapter Three

SUCCESS THROUGH APPEARANCES

(Ennea-type III)

1. Vanity, Inauthenticity and "Marketing" Orientation

Vanity is a passionate concern for one's image, or a passion of living for the eyes of others. Living for appearances implies that the focus of concern is not in one's own experience, but in the anticipation or fantasy of the experience of another, and thus the insubstantiality of the vain pursuit. Nothing could be more appropriately called "vanity of vanities" of which the preacher in Ecclesiastes speaks, than living for an ephemeral and insubstantial image (rather than out of oneself).

To speak of vanity as a living for a self-image is not different than speaking of narcissism, and indeed we may regard narcissism as a universal aspect of egoic structure, mapped on the right corner of the enneagram. Yet, since the word "narcissism" has been used in reference to more than one personality syndrome, and mostly since the publication of DSM III in reference to our ennea-type VII[1], I have not included it in this chapter heading.

---

[1] DSM III will be the abbreviation used in this book for *Diagnostic and Statistical Manual of Mental Disorders*, Third Edition, Revised (Washington, D.C.: American Psychiatric Association, 1987).

Vanity is present especially in the "hysteroid" region of the enneagram (comprising ennea-types II, III and IV), yet in the case of pride, as we have seen, it is satisfied through a combination of imaginative self-inflation and the support of selected individuals, while in ennea-type III, instead, the person mobilizes herself to "prove" objectively her value through an active implementation of the self-image in the face of a generalized other. This leads to an energetic pursuit of achievement and good form as defined by quantitative or generally accepted standards.

The difference between ennea-types III and IV lies mostly in the fact that the former identifies with the image that it "sells," while the latter is more in touch with the denigrated self-image and is thus characterized by the experience of a vanity never fulfilled. As a result, ennea-type III is cheerful, ennea-type IV depressive.

As mentioned in the introduction, Ichazo spoke of "deceit" rather than vanity as the passion of ennea-type III, relegating vanity to the sphere of the fixations. Throughout most of my teaching experience I have chosen, rather, to consider vanity as a passion akin to pride, while seeing in deception the cognitive core or fixation in ennea-type III character. The word "deceit" is not the best to evoke the particular manner of deception that goes with vanity, however—different from the lying of ennea-type II or the conning of VIII, for instance; rather than a lack of truthfulness in regard to facts (ennea-type III may be a faithful, factual reporter) there is in vanity a lack of truthfulness in regard to feelings and pretense.

In contrast to the comic vein of ennea-type II and the tragic vein of ennea-type IV, the characteristic mood of ennea-type III is one of neutrality or feeling control—where only "correct feelings" are acknowledged and expressed.

Though pride (*superbia*) and not vanity is included among the traditional capital sins of Christianity, it seems that both ideas are commonly juxtaposed—as is suggested by the common iconography that depicts pride through a woman looking at a mirror (as in Hieronymus Bosch's "Seven Deadly Sins").

It is interesting to observe that the characterological disposition involved in ennea-type III is the only one not included in DSM III—which raises the question as to whether this may be related to the fact of its constituting the modal personality in American society since the twenties. Erich Fromm addresses himself to it in his discussion of "the marketing orientation" in *Man for Himself*.[2]

2. Trait Structure

Attention Need and Vanity

If we regard the substitution of appearance for self as the fixation of ennea-type III, what are we to regard, then, as the ruling passion in this character?

It is my impression that the most characteristic emotional state and at the same time the one that underlies the characteristic interest in display to the point of self-falsification is a need for attention: a need to be seen, that was once frustrated and seeks to be satisfied through the cultivation of appearance. Other than the felt sense of wanting to be seen, heard, appreciated, there is in ennea-type III character a corresponding sense of loneliness that arises, not only from the chronic frustration of the need to be for others, but from the fact that whatever success is met with needs to be credited to a false self and to manipulation. Thus there lingers the question "would I be loved for myself if it were not for my accomplishments, my money, my pretty face, and so on?" The question is

[2] Fromm, Erich, *Man for Himself: An Inquiry into the Psychology of Ethics* (New York: Holt, Rinehart and Winston, 1964).

perpetuated by the fact that the individual is not only moved by a fear of failure in his rushing around in the pursuit of achievement, but is also plagued by fear of self-exposure and rejection if she were to reveal herself to the world without a mask.

I have included the expression "concern with appearances" in the clustering of ennea-type III descriptors along with "vanity," which not only makes reference to a passion to appear, but involves a capitulation to cultural values and a substitution of internal direction with extrinsic direction and valuation. I have also included as part of the vanity cluster, "perfectionism in regard to form," "imitativeness," and "chameleon" (in virtue of which, for instance, vanity in the counterculture may cultivate a self-image of striking lack of concern for personal appearance).

Not only a passion for the modulation of appearance is involved in the psychology of ennea-type III. A skill to the effect of achieving the aims of vanity typically supports it in the individual's psyche. Thus, beautiful women are more likely to embrace the strategy of brilliance (and the corresponding existential mistake of confusing their attractiveness with their true self). In addition to characteristics reflecting a generalized desire to please and attract, such as refinement, considerateness or generosity, some traits stand out because of their prominence which I discuss below: achievement drive, social skill and concern with personal appearance.

Achieving Orientation

Ennea-type III strives for achievement and success, and this may imply striving for wealth and for status. Since a number of traits may be understood as instrumental to this aim and drive, I will consider them under this general heading.

a) The ability to do things expeditiously and with precision is characteristic of these individuals and makes for both good secretaries and good executives. In the service of efficiency thinking tends to be precise and there is often a leaning towards mathematics. A fast tempo is also characteristic and has probably developed in the service of efficiency as well as out of a desire to stand out through special efficiency. Also in the service of efficiency is an orientation to life that is both rational and practical—an orientation often seen in the personality of those who take up engineering as a profession. Though there is interest in science, the peculiar bias of the character would be best described as scientism—that is to say, a tendency to undervalue thinking that is not logico-deductive and scientific. Along with this, one usually sees a high valuation of technology, and the broader trait of being systematic and skilled in organizing one's activities or those of others.

b) Also related to the high achievement drive is a measure of ruthlessness in human interactions when it comes to a choice between success and considerateness. Ennea-type III individuals are not only pleasers, but frequently described as cool (i.e., a "cold cookie") and calculating, and they use others as well as themselves as stepping stones to their goals.

c) Closely related to the pursuit of success are also the traits of control over self as well as over others, and dominance. These are typically observed in parents in their behavior toward their children, whom they may overpower through unsought advice and the insistence on having things done their way (even in the case of choices that would be more fitting for the children to make on their own).

d) Another important trait within this personality syndrome that stands out as a means to achievement and winning is competitiveness—a trait connected in turn to ruthlessness, to the cultivation of efficiency, and to the use of deception, bluffing, self-promotion, slander, and other behaviors discussed below under "image manipulation."

e) The traits of anxiety and tension are an understandable result of exaggerated striving for achievement and the implicit fear of failure. The rise of blood pressure in response to stress goes along with them and makes of these people the well known "ennea-type A personalities."

Social Sophistication and Skill

Another group of traits that stands out among the descriptors of ennea-type III brings together the characteristics of being entertaining, enthusiastic, bubbly, sparkling people, conversationally active, pleasing, needing applause, and witty. This generalized trait might be called "social brilliance" or "social performance." Concern with status might be regarded as an indulging motivation in these. "Tell me who you associate with, and I'll tell you who you are."

Cultivation of Sexual Attractiveness

A trait similar in nature to the previously mentioned ones are those that have to do with self-beautification and the conservation of sexual attractiveness—traits that are most specially evoked by the image of the mirror in the traditional iconography of vanity. (Generally speaking, no other women are so dependent on cosmetics as those in ennea-type III.) Just as cultivated sexual attractiveness goes hand-in-hand with frigidity, there is, more generally speaking, a special kind of vain beauty: a cold porcelain, doll-like beauty—formalistic and yet emotionally hollow.

Deceit and Image Manipulation

In the case of the three generalized traits of sexual attractiveness, social brilliance and achievement, we are in the face of different *appearances* through which the individual seeks to satisfy the thirst to be, and which at the same time veil over his existential vacuum. For while the passion to display oneself may be understood as the outgrowth of an early need for attention and validation, it can also be understood as the consequence of a confusion between being and appearance, and the corresponding confusion between extrinsic validation and intrinsic value. Since deceit is what we may call the fixation, that is, the cognitive defect in ennea-type III, I have separately grouped some descriptors that have to do more specifically with it, such as: "becoming the mask," "believing in what they sell," "affected," "false," "phony." Most characteristically, we should include deceptive emotional experience. Deception goes beyond emotional experience proper, however, for it involves rationalization and other maneuvers.

The words deception or simulation may be used as pointers to a central feature of this personality organization, used in connection with self-deception (believing in the idealized image that is presented to the world) as well as in connection with simulation before an outer audience (as in bluffing or hypocritical kindness). Yet it is the identification of the person with the role and with the mask—the loss of the sense of merely playing a role or putting on a mask—which causes what is seen by others to come to be perceived as one's reality.

Ennea-type III not only cares for appearance but has developed a skill in presentation; presenting others, presenting things and ideas. The special flair for selling and advertising that characterizes these individuals would seem to be a generalization of an ability that was originally developed in the service of "selling" and promoting themselves. Thus they not only are interested in such things as their clothing and cosmetics and exhibiting good manners, they are expert packagers of goods and information and excel in the advertising industry. The trait of promoting others, explicitly or implicitly, can be akin to a complementary one: the ability to present things or people in a bad light, to manipulate their image in an adverse way—which may be done not only through slander but also through a sophisticated social skill whereby it is possible to seem nice while back-stabbing an opponent or competitor.

Other-Directedness

Closely related to this group of traits having to do with concern about appearance and the skill in self-presentation is another having to do with the values according to which the ideal self is shaped. These are characteristically neither intrinsic nor original but external to the individual, who is the more other-directed among all the characters and has developed a skill in conducting an implicit and ongoing "marketing research" in the entourage as a point of reference for his thinking, feeling and action.

The trait of identification with prevalent values embodies both other-directedness and the chameleon quality of ennea-type III in general, i.e., its readiness to change in attitude or appearance according to fashions. Related to this other-directed characteristic, in turn, is the progressive but conservative disposition of ennea-type III—a disposition not unqualifiedly conservative, as in ennea-type IX, but a combination of conformity with a striving for progress or excellence (that results in an orientation to what is modern and avant-garde) without being radical. In practice what is both modern and what shows itself to be modern without throwing traditional values into question is scientific progress and

thus again a root of the technocratic orientation that is
so characteristic of ennea-type III psychology.

Pragmatism

Typical of ennea-type III (in contrast with the more
distinctively emotional neighbors in the enneagram) is
the characteristic conveyed through traits of rationality,
and a systematic orientation to things, also implicit in
their being described as "calculating." The expression of
these traits is not only intellectual, for the control over
self that it entails can be manifested also as being
organized and keen, practical, functional and expedient.
It is in the service of efficiency that we can understand
the more rational skills which typically give ennea-type
III an engineering or an entrepreneur mentality and
manifest also in an orientation to technology and
technocracy.

Active Vigilance

At a higher level of abstraction than both the
cognitive and behavioral sharpness or effectiveness,
there are still more general traits related to achievement
that I have called hypervigilance and activity. The
ennea-type III person is not only hypervigilant but incapable of surrender, of self-abandonment; he or she
needs to have everything under control, and has
learned early in life to cope in an attitude of self-
reliance, out of the feeling that others are not taking
care of her properly. Because of this we cannot separate
the trait of hyperactivity that makes the ennea-type III
person an "ego-go" from either stress or a deep distrust
in life—distrust that things might go well without being
in control over them. The same can apply to hyper-
vigilance; it is part of a stressful coping born of an
anxiety about things going all right and distrust in
surrendering to the "organismic self-regulation" of
one's psychomental being. The underlying lack of trust

in ennea-type III contrasts with its superficial "pollyannish" optimism (which regards everything as not only OK but wonderful) and constitutes one of the factors through which ennea-type III is prone to anxiety.

Superficiality

The trait that an outsider may describe as superficiality is in the individual's awareness more likely to manifest as a sense of not having access to the depth of her feelings, as an identity problem—in the sense of not knowing who he or she is (beyond roles and tangible characteristics) and not knowing his or her true wants (beyond those of pleasing others and being effective). Although the person may not consciously thirst after a missing depth, the presence of dis-satisfaction is apparent in the very intensity of the rushing for accomplishment or the labors taken to be pleasing and acceptable. To the extent that the thirst for being is displaced into an outer search, the individual does not allow the opportunity even to acknowledge it—thus perpetuating the chronic error.

3. Existential Psychodynamics

Just as in the schizoid character the existential issue is most apparent to the subject—who is keenly aware of the experience of inner emptiness—it is in ennea-type III character that the existential issue of an inner vacuum is most observable to *outsiders*, who typically see vain persons as superficial, empty, or "plastic." This tendency of the vain to ignore the impoverishment of their experiential world brings them close to ennea-type IX in which, as we will see, ontic obscuration—through its very centrality—is most ignoring of itself. Their similarity in this regard fits the relationship between them on the enneagram according to which vain

E.J. Gold, *Model In Studio,*
sumi-e, 9" x 12".

identification with appearance is the psychodynamic root of pathological self-forgetfulness.

When aware of "something missing inside" an ennea-type III person is likely to verbalize this perception of emptiness as a not knowing who he or she is—i.e., an identity problem. The wide recognition of the identity issue together with the sense of its universality reflects, I think, the prevalence of ennea-type III in American culture.

What "not knowing who I am" generally means in an ennea-type III individual is, "All I know is the role that I enact—is there something else besides?" The individual has come to realize that his life is a series of performances and that identity has rested thus far in identification with professional status and other roles. Together with realizing "this is not me" or "these roles don't amount to anybody" there is a sense of being out of touch with some hidden or potential self. Along with an intuition of an ignored self or individuality, there is usually, also, the sense of not knowing one's true wishes and feelings—a sense that dawns upon them to the extent that they begin to recognize fabricated feelings, and the extent to which choices are not inner directed but supported in outer models.

While in more socially-oriented individuals there is a "butterfly" quality to their status-seeking drivenness and it is obvious that their self-alienation has resulted from an excessive concern with the image that they sell in face of the public eye, in the more sexually oriented ones an equivalent process takes place in regard to the search for "sexual applause" behind the cultivation of what we call sex-appeal. The passion to please and attract polarizes the attention of the person, here too, towards the surface of her being at the expense of focus on the depth of erotic and emotional experience—bringing along the frequent complication of frigidity in women.

Jodorowsky has given a profound account of the situation in an essay on a sexual superman who has hundreds of hands and thousands of fingers in each of which there is a sexual organ or a tongue, who can achieve the highest standards of sexual performance, yet whose focus on effectiveness tragically leaves him with no attention left to enjoy.[3]

Given the prominence of the existential issue in ennea-type III (which is understandable in view of its place in the enneagram) it is useful to go beyond the interpretation of the passion for applause as a substitute for love or as the indirect expression of a love wish. True as that may be and important to acknowledge, I think we need to consider that the chronic struggle of ennea-type III to obtain "narcissistic supplies" is supported by the self-created impoverishment that arises precisely from the diversion of psychic energy towards performance and living through the eyes of others (and thus in an imaginary "movie").

Due consideration of the way in which the frantic agitation of "ego-go" creates the loss of being which, in turn, fuels the search for being in the realm of appearances, cannot be without consequences, for, if it is true that truth can set us free, true insight in this vicious circle can liberate the individual's energy and attention to focus on the commonly avoided — and potentially painful — interiority.

In his frantic agitation in pursuit of achievement, status or applause, and in the corresponding inability to pause to look within, the ennea-type III person seems to be repeating to himself that very American injunction "Don't just stand there, do something." Correspondingly he needs to be told "Don't just do something, *stand* there."

It is important also for psychotherapists to understand that these people who usually have difficulty in

---

[3] "La vida sexual del hombre elástico." In *Metal*, No. 47 (Spain).

being alone and in extricating themselves from over-acting achievement can particularly benefit from the task of facing themselves and from bearing the "loss of face" entailed by not looking into the social mirror.

Because interiority is so foreign to them, something seemingly not existing in a world where only form and quantity exist, meditation, particularly meditation that emphasizes non-doing, may seem most uninteresting and meaningless to them. Through closer observation of this meaninglessness of "just sitting" with enough intellectual conviction or personal trust to engage in the task, however, it is possible that further focus on boredom or meaninglessness might lead to some perception of the tragedy of an incapacity to be nourished through a living sense of existence.

Chapter Four

SEEKING HAPPINESS
THROUGH PAIN

(Ennea-type IV)

1. Envy and the Masochistic Personality

The emotional state of envy involves a painful sense of lack and a craving towards that which is felt lacking; the situation involves a sense of goodness as something outside oneself that needs to be incorporated.

Though an understandable reaction to early frustration and deprivation, envy constitutes a self-frustrating factor in the psyche, for the excessive craving for love that it entails never answers the chronic sense of inner scarcity and badness, but on the contrary, stimulates further frustration and pain.

The position of envy in the enneagram is that of a satellite to vanity and a neighbor to point 5, avarice, which entails a comparable sense of deprivation to envy, though it involves a different attitude in face of the experience of scarcity. While point 4 represents a forceful reaching out, an intense demand for that which is missed, point 5 is characterized by a psychic attitude of giving up the expectation of anything from the outside and, rather, a concern about holding in one's energy, caring and attention.

The connection with vanity is even more important than the one to avarice, since point 4 constitutes a member of the triad in the right corner of the enneagram, which, as a whole, gravitates around an excessive concern with the image of the self. While an ennea-type III person identifies with that part of the self that coincides with the idealized image, the ennea-type IV individual identifies with that part of the psyche that *fails* to fit the idealized image, and is always striving to achieve the unattainable. Here is a person animated by a vanity that fails to reach its goal because of the admixture in it of a sense of scarcity and worthlessness (of point 5).

Even though the ennea-types mapped at the positions 4 and 5 (envy and avarice) have in common the sense of worthlessness, guilt and lack, and both may be described as depressed, they are in marked contrast in various regards. While guilt in envy is conscious torture, in avarice it is partially veiled over by a seeming moral indifference (that it shares with ennea-type VIII and constitutes a rebellion against its own excessive demands and accusations); while depression in envy manifests as overt grief, the avaricious often have trouble in crying or contacting their pain, so that their depression manifests, rather, as apathy and a sense of emptiness. It may be said that ennea-type V is a "dry" depression contrary to the "wet" depression of ennea-type IV: just as avarice is resigned, envy is passionate. In this is reflected a sharply differentiated feature: dry avarice is apathetic, wet envy, most intense; if the one is a desert, the other is a marsh. (The French use of *envie* to mean 'desire' underscores the implicit observation that envy is the most passionate of passions.) While ennea-type V involves an internal atmosphere of quietness, ennea-type IV involves an atmosphere of turmoil and turbulence. The most characteristic aspect of ennea-type IV character besides envious motivation may be seen in the tendency to self-victimization and frustration.

2. Trait Structure

Envy

If we understand the essence of envy as an excessively intense desire for incorporation of the "good mother," the concept coincides with the psychoanalytic notion of a "cannibalistic impulse" which may manifest not only as a love hunger, but as a more generalized voraciousness or greediness.

Whether we agree or not with Melanie Klein in regard to the envious fantasies that she attributes to the infant at the breast,[1] I think that it is reasonable to take them as a symbolic expression of experiences in the adult—and, more particularly, the characteristic process of self-frustration that seems inseparable from envy, as the ongoing basis of its over-desiring characteristic. Whatever the truth about the beginnings of envy during breastfeeding, too, in the experience of many envy is not consciously experienced in connection with the mother but towards a preferred sibling, so that the individual has sought to be her or him rather than himself in the pursuit of parental love. Often there is an element of sexual envy that Freud observed in women and—from the point of view of his sexual and bio-logistic interpretation—branded as "penis envy." Since envy of women is also experienced by some men in distinctly erotic terms we might also speak of "vagina envy"—though I am of the opinion that sexual fantasies are derivative from a more basic phenomenon of gender-envy involving a sense of the superiority of the other sex. Given the patriarchal bias of our civilization it is no wonder that envy of the male is more common (and, indeed, ennea-type IV women loom large in the liberation movement) but both forms of sexual envy are striking in the case of the counter-sexual identification

[1] *Envy and Gratitude* (London: Tavistock, 1957).

underlying homosexuality and lesbianism (both of them more frequent in ennea-type IV than in any other character).

Another realm of expression of envy is social, and can manifest both as an idealization of the upper classes and a strong social climbing drive, as Proust has portrayed in *Remembrance of Things Past*, or, alternatively, as hateful competitiveness toward the privileged (as portrayed by Stendhal in *The Red and the Black*). Still more subtly, envy can manifest as an ever present pursuit of the extraordinary and the intense, along with the corresponding dissatisfaction with the ordinary and non-dramatic.

A primitive pathological manifestation of the same disposition is the symptom of bulimia, which I have observed to exist in the context of ennea-type IV character; many people experience a subtle echo of that condition: occasional feelings of painful emptiness at the pit of the stomach.

Whereas avarice and, most characteristically, anger are hidden traits in the personality syndromes of which they are part (since they have been compensated by pathological detachment and reactive traits of benignity and dignity, respectively) in the case of envy the passion itself is apparent, and the person thus suffers from the contradiction between an extreme neediness and the taboo against it. Also in light of this clash between the perception of intense envy and the corresponding sense of shamefulness and vileness in being envious we can understand the "bad image" trait discussed below.

Poor Self-image

The most striking of traits from the point of view of the number of descriptors in it is that which conveys a poor self-concept. Included among the specific characteristics are not only "bad self-image" itself, but others such as "feeling inadequate," "prone to shame," "sense of ridicule," "feeling unintelligent," "ugly," "repulsive," "rotten," "poisonous" and so on. Even though I have chosen to speak of "poor self-image" separately, (thus reflecting the appearance of an independent conceptual cluster of descriptors) it is impossible to dissociate the phenomenon of envy from this bad self-image, which object relations theorists interpret as the consequence of the introjection of a "bad object." It is such self-denigration that creates the "hole" out of which arises the voracity of envy proper in its clinging, demanding, biting, dependent, overattached manifestations.

Focus on Suffering

I still have not commented upon the cluster of traits usually designated by the label "masochistic." In the understanding of these we should invoke, beyond the suffering that arises through a poor self-image and the frustration of exaggerated neediness, the use of pain as vindictiveness and an unconscious hope of obtaining love through suffering. Ennea-type IV individuals, as a result of these dynamic factors and also of a basic emotional disposition are not only sensitive, intense, passionate, and romantic, but tend to suffer from loneliness and may harbor a tragic sense of their life or life in general.

Possessed of a deep longing, dominated by nostalgia, intimately forlorn and sometimes visibly liquid-eyed and languorous, they are usually pessi- mistic, often bitter and sometimes cynical. Associated traits are lamenting, complaining, despondent and self-pitying. Of particular prominence in the painful landscape of ennea-type IV psychology is what has to do with the feeling of loss, usually the echo of real experiences of loss and deprivation, sometimes present as a fear of future loss and particularly manifest as a proneness to suffering intensely from the separations and frustrations of life. Particularly striking is the propensity of ennea-type IV to the mourning response, not only in relation to persons but also pets. It is in this cluster, I think, that we are closest to the core of the character ennea-type, and particularly in the maneuver that it entails of focusing upon and expressing suffering to obtain love.

Just as it is a functional aspect of crying, in the human infant, to attract mother's protective care, I think the experience of crying contains that of seeking attention. Just as ennea-type III children learn to shine to get attention (and those who will develop the ennea-type V or ennea-type VIII character, hopeless about ever getting it, prefer the way of withdrawal or the way of power), here the individual learns to get "negative" attention through the intensification of need—which operates not only in a histrionic manner (through the imaginative amplification of suffering and the amplification of the expression of suffering), but also through walking into painful situations—i.e., through a painful life course. Crying may be, indeed, not only a pain, but a satisfaction for an ennea-type IV individual. It remains to say that (as the word "masochistic" brings to mind) there can be a sad sweetness in suffering. It feels real, though it is also the opposite—for the main self-deception in ennea-type IV is exaggerating a position of victimization, which goes hand-in-hand with their "claiming," demanding dis-position.[2]

---

[2] Silvano Arietti, "Affective Disorders" in *American Handbook of Psychiatry*, Volume III, Silvano Arietti, Editor-in-Chief (New York: Basic Books, 1974). Arietti has proposed precisely this expression "claiming" for the most common personality background of neurotic depression (in contrast to that of psychotic depression, which we will discuss in connection to ennea-type IX).

"Moving Toward"

More than those of any other character, ennea-type IV individuals can be called "love addicted," and their craving for love is in turn supported by a need of the acknowledgement that they are unable to give themselves. "Dependency"—its corollary—can manifest not only as a clinging to relationships that are frustrating, but as an adhesiveness—a subtle imposition of contact which seems the outcome of not only a contact need, but an anticipated defense or postponement of separation. Related to the craving for care is also the commonly observed "helplessness" of ennea-type IV individuals, which, as in ennea-type V, manifests as a motivational inability to care properly for themselves and may be interpreted as an unconscious maneuver to attract protection. The need for financial protection, specifically, may be supported by the desire to feel cared for.

Nurturance

Ennea-type IV people are usually considered thoughtful, understanding, apologetic, soft, gentle, cordial, self-sacrificing, humble, sometimes obsequious. Their nurturant quality not only appears to constitute a form of "giving to get," i.e., dependent on the love need alone, but on an empathic identification with the needs of others which sometimes causes them to be concerned parents, empathetic social workers, attentive psychotherapists and fighters for the underdog. The nurturant characteristic of ennea-type IV can be dynamically understood as a form of seduction in the service of the intense need of the other and its painful frustration. Caring for others may be masochistically exaggerated to a point of self-enslavement, and contributes thus to the self-frustration and pain that in turn activates the demanding and litigious aspects of the character.

Emotionality

The word "emotional," though implicit in a high level of suffering, deserves to be placed by itself in view of the determining contribution of feeling-dominance to the structure of ennea-type IV character. We are in the presence of an "emotional ennea-type," just as in the case of ennea-type II, only here with a greater admixture of intellectual interests and introversion. (Indeed, these are the two kinds of character most properly regarded as emotional, for the word applies to them more exactly than it does in the case of the cheerful and helpful seductiveness of gluttons, and the defensive warmth of the more outwardly fearful and dependent cowards.) The quality of intense emotionality applies not only to the romantic feelings, the dramatization of suffering and to the love addicted and nurturant characteristics, but also to the expression of anger. Envious people feel hate intensely, and their screams are the most impressive. Also found in ennea-types II and III, at the right corner of the enneagram, is that quality that psychiatry has called "plasticity" in reference to a capacity to role-play (related to the capacity to modulate the expression of feelings).

Competitive Arrogance

Connected to a hateful emotionality, an attitude of superiority sometimes exists along with—and in compensation for—a bad self-image. Though the individual may seethe in self-deprecation and self-hate, the attitude to the outer world is in this case that of a "prima-donna," or at least a very special person. When this claim of specialness is frustrated it may be complicated by a victimized role of "misunderstood genius." In line with this development, individuals also develop traits of wit, interesting conversation, and others in which a natural disposition towards imaginativeness, analysis or emotional depth (for instance) are secondarily put to the service of the contact need and the desire to summon admiration.

Refinement

An inclination to refinement (and the corresponding aversion to grossness) is manifest in descriptors such as "stylish," "delicate," "elegant," "tasteful," "artistic," "sensitive" and sometimes "arty" and "affected," "mannered" and "posturing." They may be understood as efforts on the part of the person to compensate for a poor self-image (so that an ugly self-image and the refined self-ideal may be seen as reciprocally supporting each other); also, they convey an attempt on the part of the person to be something different from what he or she is, perhaps connected to class envy. The lack of originality entailed by such imitativeness in turn perpetuates an envy of originality—just as the attempt to imitate original individuals and the wish to emulate spontaneity are doomed to fail.

Artistic Interests

The characteristic inclination of ennea-type IV towards the arts is over-determined: at least one of its roots lies in the refined characteristic of envious character. It is supported too, by the feeling-centered disposition of the ennea-type. Other components are the possibility of idealizing pain through art and even transmuting it—to the extent that it becomes an element in the configuration of beauty.

Strong Superego

Refinement is perhaps the most characteristic of ways in which ennea-type IV seeks to be better than he or she is, and in so doing exercises discipline. More generally, there is a typically strong superego that the ennea-type IV character shares with ennea-type I, but on the whole, ennea-type IV is more keenly aware of his or her standards and his or her ego ideal is more aesthetic than ethical. Along with discipline (which may reach a masochistic degree) the superego characteristic of ennea-type IV involves descriptors of tenacity and of being rule-oriented. Love of ceremony reflects both the aesthetic-refined and the rule-oriented characteristics. A strong superego is, of course, involved in the guilt propensity of ennea-type IV, in its shame, self-hate and self-denigration.

3. Existential Psychodynamics

While we have good reason to believe that the pattern of envy originates in frustration of the child's early attachment needs, and we may understand the chronic pain in this character as a residue of the pain of the past, it is useful to consider that it may also be a trap for ennea-type IV individuals to get stuck in lamenting over the past. Also, while it is very true that it was love that the child needed urgently and sought, the exaggerated and compulsive search for love *in the present* may be regarded as a disfunction and only a mirage or approximate interpretation of what the adult is in dire need of. This, rather than outer support, acknowledgement and care, is the ability to acknowledge, support and love him- or herself; and also the development of a sense of self as center that might counteract the "ex-centric" expectation of goodness from the outside.

We may envision ennea-type IV psychology precisely from the point of view of an impoverishment of being or selfhood that envy seeks to "fill up" and which is, in turn, perpetuated through self-denigration, through the search for being through love and through the emulation of others ("I am like Einstein, therefore I

E.J. Gold, *The Ghost Inside*,
pastel, 12" x 12", 1955.

exist"). The ennea-type IV psyche functions as if it had concluded early in life "I am not loved therefore I am worthless" and now pursues worthiness through the love that was once missing (love me so I know I am all right), and through a process of self-refining distortion—through the pursuit of something different and presumably better and nobler than what he or she is.

These processes are self-frustrating, for love, once obtained, is likely to be invalidated ("he cannot be worthwhile if he loves me") or, having stimulated neurotic claims, leads to frustration and also invalidation on that basis; yet, more basically, the pursuit of being through the emulation of the self-ideal stands on a basis of self-rejection and of blindness to the value of one's true self (just as the pursuit of the extraordinary involves denigration of the ordinary). Because of this, ennea-type IV needs, in addition to insight into these traps, and more than any other character, the development of self-support: the self-support that comes, ultimately, from appreciative awareness and the sense of dignity of self and of life in all of its forms.

There is a pathology of values entailed in envy that may be explained in light of the metaphor (which I find in Arcipreste de Hita's *Book Of Good Love*)[3] of a dog that carries a bone and who, believing his reflection upon a pool to be another dog with a more desirable bone, opens his jaws as he lunges for it, losing in the process the bone he has. We may say: the reflection of a bone has no "being," just as there is no being in either idealized or deprecated self-images.

---

[3] *Libro de Buen Amor*, ed. by Maria Brey Mariño (Madrid: Editorial Castalia, 1982).

SPY

Chapter Five

SEEKING WHOLENESS THROUGH ISOLATION

(Ennea-type V)

1. Avarice and Pathological Detachment

As a spiritual "missing of the mark" or spiritual hindrance, avarice must have naturally been understood by the church fathers in more than its literal sense, and so we see confirmed in Chaucer's "The Parson's Tale" from The Canterbury Tales, a reflection of the spirit of his time: "Avarice consists not only of greed for lands and chattles, but sometimes for learning and for glory."[1]

If the gesture of anger is to run over, that of avarice is one of holding back and holding in. While anger expresses greed in an assertive (even though unacknowledged) way, greed in avarice manifests only through retentiveness. This is a fearful grasping, implying a fantasy that letting go would result in catastrophic depletion. Behind the hoarding impulse there is, we may say, an experience of impending impoverishment.

Yet, holding on is only half of ennea-type V psychology; the other half is giving up too easily. Because of an excessive resignation in regard to love

---

[1] op. cit., p. 595

and people precisely, there is a compensatory clutching at oneself—which may or may not manifest in a grasping onto possessions, but involves a much more generalized hold over one's inner life as well as an economy of effort and resources. The holding back and self-control of avarice is not unlike that of the anger ennea-type, yet it is accompanied by a getting stuck through clutching at the present without openness to the emerging future.

Just as it can be said of the wrathful that they are mostly unconscious of their anger and that anger is their main taboo—it may be said of the avaricious that their avarice is mostly unconscious, while consciously they may feel every gesture of possession and drawing up of boundaries as forbidden. It might be said that the avaricious is internally perfectionistic rather than critical to the outer world, but most importantly the difference between the two ennea-types lies in the contrast between the active extroversion of the former and the introversion of the latter (the introversion of a thinking ennea-type that avoids action).

Also ennea-type I is demanding while ennea-type V seeks to minimize his own needs and claims, and is prone to be pushed around in virtue of a compulsive obedience. Though both ennea-types are characterized by a strong superego, they are like cops and robbers respectively, for the former identifies more with its idealized superego-congruent self, while ennea-type V identifies with the overwhelmed and guilty subpersonality that is the object of superegoic demands.

Ichazo's word for the fixation corresponding to ennea-type V is "stinginess," which stands, I think, too close to "avarice"—the ruling passion or emotion. "Meanness" with its connotation of an unknowing failure to give would come closer to capturing the dominant aspect of the ennea-type V strategy in face of the world: self-distancing and the giving up of relationships. Still better, however, is to speak of being detached, withdrawn, autistic and schizoid.

2. Trait Structure

Retentiveness

As usual, it is possible to find in this character a cluster of descriptors corresponding to the dominant passion. In it, along with avarice, belong such characteristics as lack of generosity in matters of money, energy and time, and also meanness—with its implication of an insensitivity to the needs of others. Among the characteristics of retentiveness it is important to take note of a holding on to the ongoing content of the mind, as if wanting to elaborate or extract the last drop of significance—a characteristic that results in a typical jerkiness of mental function, a subtle form of rigidity that militates against the individual's openness to environmental stimulation and to what is emerging, the transition of the present mental state to the next. This is the characteristic which von Gebsattel has pointed out in "ananchastics" as a "getting stuck."[2]

We may say that the implicit interpersonal strategy of holding on implies a preference for self-sufficiency in regard to resources instead of approaching others. This, in turn, involves a pessimistic outlook in regard to the prospect of either receiving care and protection or in having the power to demand or take what is needed.

Not Giving

Also the avoidance of commitment can be considered as an expression of not giving since it amounts to an avoidance of giving in the future. In this

[2] V.E. von Gebsattel, "The World of the Compulsive" in *Existence: A New Dimension in Psychiatry and Psychology*, edited by Rollo May (New York: Basic Books, 1959).

avoidance of commitment, however, there is also another aspect: the need of ennea-type V individuals to be completely free, unbound, unobstructed, in possession of the fullness of themselves—a trait representing a composite of avarice and an over-sensitivity to engulfment (to be discussed later). It may be pointed out that hoarding implies not just avarice, but a projection of avarice into the future—a protection against being left without. Here, again, the trait represents a derivation not only from avarice, but from the intense need of autonomy of the character (see below).

Pathological Detachment

Given the reciprocity of giving and taking in human relationships, a compulsion to not give (surely the echo of perceiving in early life that it goes against survival to give more than is received) can hardly be sustained except at the expense of relationship itself—as if the individual considered: "If the only way to hold on to the little I have is to distance myself from others and their needs or wants, that is what I will do."

An aspect of pathological detachment is the characteristic aloofness of ennea-type V; another, the quality of being a "loner," i.e., one accustomed to being solitary and who, out of resignation in regard to relating, does not feel particularly lonely. Seclusiveness is, of course, part of the broader trait of detachment, since it requires emotional detachment and repression of the need to relate, to be in isolation. The difficulty that ennea-type V individuals have in making friends may be considered also here, for an important aspect of this difficulty is the lack of motivation to relate.

Though it is easy to see how detachment can arise as a complication of retentiveness, the giving up of relationship is interdependent with the inhibition of needs—for it could hardly be compatible to give up relationships and to be needy, and thus giving up

relationship already implies a relinquishment or mini-
mization of needs. While resignation in regard to one's
own needs is practically a corollary of detachment, the
inhibition of the expression of anger in this character
involves not only resignation in regard to love needs,
but also the fear that is present in the schizoid
personality in virtue of its position next to the left
corner of the enneagram.

Fear of Engulfment

The fear and avoidance of being "swallowed up by
others" might be a corollary of the avoidance of
relationships, yet not only this, for it is also the
expression of a half-conscious perception of one's own
suppressed need to relate, and (as Fairbairn has
emphasized) a fear of potential dependency. The great
sensitivity to interference and interruption of ennea-
type V individuals is not only the expression of a
detached attitude, but a function of the person's
proneness to interrupt herself in the face of external
demands and perceived needs of others. In other words,
a great sensitivity to interference goes hand-in-hand
with an over-docility, in virtue of which the individual
interferes all too easily with her own spontaneity, with
her preferences and with acting in a way coherent with
her needs in the presence of others. Also, in light of this
over-docility (understandable as a by-product of a
strong repressed love need) we can understand the
particular emphasis on aloneness in ennea-type V. To
the extent that the relationship entails alienation from
one's own preferences and authentic expression there
arises an implicit stress and the need to recover from it:
a need to find oneself again in aloneness.

Autonomy

The great need for autonomy is an understandable
corollary of giving up relationships. Together with

developing the "distance machinery" (to use H.S. Sullivan's expression), the individual needs to be able to do without external supplies. One who cannot get to others to satisfy his desires needs to build up his resources, stocking them up, so to say, inside his ivory tower. Closely related to autonomy and yet a trait on its own is the idealization of autonomy which reinforces the repression of desires and underlies a life-philosophy much like that which Hesse puts in Siddhartha's mouth: "I can think, I can wait, I can fast."[3]

Feelinglessness

Though I have already alluded to a repression of needs and mentioned the suppression of anger in ennea-type V, it seems desirable to group these descriptors along with others in a more generalized trait of feelinglessness. It has to do with the loss of awareness of feelings and even an interference with the generation of feeling, which results from the avoidance of expression and action. This characteristic makes some individuals indifferent, cold, unempathic and apathetic. Also anhedonia might be placed here, though the greater or lesser incapacity to enjoy pleasure is a more complex phenomenon: while ennea-type I is aversive to pleasure, ennea-type V simply appears as having a diminished capacity to experience it. In this is implicit, however, the fact that pleasure does not rank high in the scale of values of this character for it is postponed to more "urgent" drives, such as the drive to keep a safe distance from others and the drive for autonomy.

Postponement of Action

We may say that to act is to invest oneself, to put one's energies into use, which goes against the grain of retentive orientation of ennea-type V. Yet, more

[3] Herman Hesse, *Siddhartha* (New York: New Directions, 1951).

generally, action cannot be considered as separate from interaction, so when the drive to relate is low the drive to do is concomitantly lessened. On the other hand, action requires an enthusiasm for something, a presence of feelings—which is not the case in the apathetic individual. To do is also something like showing one's self to the world, for one's actions manifest one's intentions. One who wants to keep his intentions hidden (as the avaricious typically does) will also inhibit his activity on these grounds and develop, instead of a spontaneous movement and initiative, an excessive restraint. The characteristic trait of procrastination may be regarded as a hybrid between negativism and the avoidance of action.

Cognitive Orientation

Ennea-type V is not only introversive (as is implied in moving away from relationships) but also typically intellectual (as introverts generally tend to be). Through a predominantly cognitive orientation the individual may seek substitute satisfaction—as in the replacement of living through reading. Yet the symbolic replacement of life is not the only form of expression of intense thinking activity: another aspect is the preparation for life—a preparation that is intense to the extent that the individual never feels ready enough. In the elaboration of perceptions as preparation for (inhibited) action, the activity of abstraction is particularly striking. Ennea-type V individuals lean towards the activity of classification and organization, and not only display a strong attraction towards the process of ordering experience, but tend to dwell in abstractions while at the same time avoiding concreteness. This avoidance of concreteness, in turn, is linked to the ennea-type's hiddenness: only the results of one's perceptions are offered to the world, not its raw material.

Related to abstraction and the organization of experience is an interest in science and a curiosity in regard to knowledge. Also the inhibition of feelings and of action, along with the emphasis of cognition gives rise to the characteristic of being a mere witness of life, a non-attached yet keen observer of it, who in this very keenness seems to be seeking to replace life through its understanding.

Sense of Emptiness

Naturally, the suppression of feelings and the avoidance of life (in the interest of avoiding feelings) constitutes the avoidance of action along with an objective impoverishment of experience. We may understand the sense of sterility, depletion and meaninglessness that are typical of ennea-type V as the result of an objective impoverishment in the life of relatedness, feeling and doing. The prevalence of such a sense of inner vacuum in modern times (when other symptomatic neuroses have been relatively eclipsed by the "existential ones") reflects the proportion of ennea-type V individuals in the consulting rooms of psychotherapists today. One psychodynamic consequence of this existential pain of feeling faintly existing is the attempt to compensate for the impoverishment of feeling and active life through the intellectual life (for which the individual is usually well endowed constitutionally) and through being a curious and/or critical "outsider." Another more fundamental consequence, however, is the fact of "ontic insufficiency" in stimulating the dominant passion itself—as is the case in each one of the character structures.

Guilt

Ennea-type V (along with ennea-type IV, at the bottom of the enneagram) is characterized by guilt proneness—even though in ennea-type IV guilt is more intensely felt—is "buffered" by a generalized distancing from feelings.

Guilt manifests in a vague sense of inferiority however, in a vulnerability to intimidation, in a sense of awkwardness and self-consciousness, and, most typically, in the very characteristic hiddenness of the person. Though guilt can be understood in light of the strong superego of ennea-type V, I believe that it is also a consequence of the early implicit decision of the person to withdraw love (as a response to the lovelessness of the outer world). The cold detachment of ennea-type V may thus be regarded as an equivalent to the anger of the vindictive ennea-type (VIII), who sets out to go it alone and fights for his needs in a hostile world. His moving away from people is an equivalent to moving against, as if, in the impossibility to express anger, he annihilated the other in his inner world. In embracing an attitude of loveless disregard, he thus feels a guilt that is not only comparable to that of the tough-minded bully, but more "visible" since in the bully it is defensively denied, while here it manifests as a pervasive and Kafkaesque guilt proneness.

High Superego

The trait of high superego may be regarded as interdependent with guilt: the superego's demanding results in guilt and is a compensatory response to it (not unlike the reaction formation involved in the high superego of ennea-type I). Like the ennea-type I individual, ennea-type V feels driven, and demands much out of himself as well as of others. It may be said that ennea-type I is more externally perfectionistic, ennea-type V internally so. Also, the former holds on to a relative identification with his superego, while the latter identifies with his inner "underdog."

Negativism

A source trait related to the perception of the needs of others as binding, and also a form of rebellion against one's own (superegoic) demands, is that which involves, beyond an avoidance of interference or influence, a wish to *subvert* the perceived demands of others and of oneself. Here we can see again a factor underlying the characteristic postponement of action, for sometimes this involves a wish *not* to do that which is perceived as a should, a wish not to "give" something requested or expected, even when the source of the request is internal rather than societal. A manifestation of such negativism is that anything that the individual chooses to do on the basis of true desire is likely to become, once an explicit project, a "should" that evokes a loss of motivation through internal rebellion.

Hypersensitivity

Though we have surveyed the insensitive aspect of ennea-type V, we also need to include its characteristic hypersensitivity, manifest in traits ranging from a low tolerance of pain to fear of rejection.

It is my impression that this trait is more basic (in the sense of being psychodynamically fundamental) than that of feelinglessness and that, as Kretschmer[4] has proposed, emotional dullness sets in precisely as a defense against the hypersensitive characteristic. The hypersensitive characteristic of ennea-type V involves a sense of weakness, a vulnerability and also a sensitivity in dealing with the world of objects and even persons. To the extent that the individual is not autistically disconnected from the perception of others, he is gentle, soft and harmless. Even in his dealing with the

---

4) Ernst Kretschmer, *Physique and Character: An Investigation of the Nature of Constitution and of the Theory of Temperament* (New York: Cooper Square, 1936)

inanimate environment this is true: he does not want to
disturb the way things are; he would like, so to say, to
walk without harming the grass on which he treads.
Though this hypersensitive characteristic may be
ascribed, together with the cognitive orientation and
introversive moving away from people, to the
cerebrotonic background of the ennea-type, we can also
understand it as partly derived from the experience of
half-conscious psychological pain: the pain of guilt, the
pain of unacknowledged loneliness, the pain of
emptiness. It seems to me that an individual who feels
full and substantial can stand more pain than one who
feels empty.

Lack of pleasure and the feeling of insignificance,
thus, would seem to influence the limit of pain that can
be accepted, and hypersensitivity itself, no doubt,
stands as a factor behind the individual's decision to
avoid the pain of frustrating relationships through the
choice of isolation and autonomy.

3. Existential Psychodynamics

While it makes much sense to view the schizoid
disposition as a withdrawal in the face of assumed
lovelessness, and it is useful to take into account the fact
that the sense of lovelessness continues to exist not only
as a "phantom pain" but as a result of the fact that a
basic distrust leads him to invalidate the positive
feelings of others towards him as manipulative—I think
that a whole new therapeutic vista opens up when we
take into account the repercussions of an emptiness
which the individual inadvertently creates precisely
through the attempt to fill it up. Thus we may say that
it is not just mother love that the adult ennea-type V is
needing right now, but true aliveness, the sense of
existing, a plenitude that he sabotages from moment to

E.J. Gold, *Your Royal Majesty,*
pastel and pencil, 11" x 15", 1987.

moment through the compulsive avoidance of life and relationship.

Thus it is not in receiving love that lies his greatest hope (particularly since he cannot trust other people's feelings) but in his own ability to love and relate.

Just as inwardness is animated by a thirst for enrichment and ends up in impoverishment, so also a misplaced search for being perpetuates ontic obscuration. The self-absorbed schizoid would remove himself away from the interfering world; yet in the act of thus removing himself, he also removes himself from himself.

An implicit assumption in ennea-type V is that being is to be found only beyond the realm of becoming: away from the body, away from the feelings, away from thinking itself. (And so it is—yet with a "but"; for it can only be realized by one who is *not avoiding* the body, the feelings and the mind.)

While it is easy to understand grasping as a complication of ontic thirst, it may be well to dwell on how grasping is also—together with avoidance—at its source. The process is conveyed by the story of Midas, who in his wish for riches, wished that whatever he touched turned into gold. The unanticipated tragic consequences of his wish—the turning into gold of his daughter—symbolizes, better than conceptual thinking alone can convey, the process by which reaching for the most valuable can entail a dehumanization—and reaching for the extraordinary, an impoverishment in the capacity to value the ordinary.

Chapter Six

THE PERSECUTED PERSECUTOR

(Ennea-type VI)

1. Fear and Suspiciousness

Ichazo's words for the passion and the fixation of ennea-type VI, as mentioned in the Introduction, were "timidity" and "cowardice" respectively.

Timidity may be taken to mean an anxious hesitation or inhibition of action in the presence of fear, but if this is so, then the meaning is not different from that of "fear" which I am using to designate the ruling passion in this character.

If we use fear or cowardice to designate the ruling passion of ennea-type VI, however, we need to point out, as in the case of anger and other emotions, that this important state need not be directly manifested in behavior. It may be, alternatively, manifest in the over-compensation of a conscious attitude of heroic striving. The counterphobic denial of fear is no different in essence from the covering up of anger through excessive gentleness and control, the covering up of selfishness through excessive yielding, and other forms of compensation manifested throughout the range of characters, particularly in some of the sub-ennea-types.

More characteristic than fear and cowardice may be, in many ennea-type VI individuals, the presence of anxiety—that derivative of fear that might be characterized as fear without the perception of external or internal danger.

Even though fear is not among the "deadly sins," the transcendence of fear may be a cornerstone of the true Christian ideal inasmuch as this involves an *Imitatio Christi* to a point that is necessarily heroic. It is interesting to observe, however, that the Christian ideal shifted from that of the early martyrs to one pervaded by attitudes which Nietszche criticized under the epithet of "slave morality" (though lately, in South America at least, the church has become heroic again to the point of martyrdom).

Unlike the Greek notion of virtue (*arete*) which emphasized courage, as Nietszche pointed out, the ideal of Christian society supports an excessive obedience to authority and an unbalance in the direction of Apollonian control over Dionysian expansiveness.

Just as we may witness a degradation in Christian consciousness along the specific path of courage to cowardice, we may speak of a degradation in its understanding of faith. While faith is, in the body of fourth way ideas, the psychocatalyst that lies as a gate of potential liberation from the bondage of insecurity, this is an altogether different thing from what the word has come to mean in average religious discourse: a firm holding on to a set of beliefs.

As I will elaborate upon in the psychodynamic analysis, I think that the cognitive counterpart of fear may be found in an attitude of self-invalidation, self-opposition and self-blaming—a becoming an enemy to oneself—that seems to imply that it is better to oppose oneself (siding with anticipated opposition outside) than to meet an outer enemy. The DSM III definition of paranoid character is narrower than ennea-type VI, which involves three different varieties of paranoid thinking according to the way of dealing with anxiety. The phobic character of psychoanalysis, now echoed in the DSM III "avoidant personality" is another, and also a more obsessive style usually diagnosed as a mixed personality disorder, between the paranoid and the obsessive.

2. Trait Structure

Fear, Cowardice and Anxiety

A central characteristic among the descriptive traits of ennea-type VI is the peculiar emotion that contemporary psychology has described as anxiety. This may be likened to a frozen fear or a frozen alarm before danger that has ceased to threaten (though it continues to be imagined).

Examining ennea-type VI descriptors I find, aside from anxiety, many in which fear is the explicit psychological characteristic: fear of change, fear of making mistakes, fear of the unknown, fear of letting go, fear of hostility and trickery, fear of not being able to cope, fear of not surviving, fear of aloneness in a threatening world, fear of betrayal, and fear of loving. Paranoid jealousy might be included in the same group.

Closely connected to these are the traits that have to do with the expression of fear in behavior: insecurity, hesitation, indecision and tentativeness (a consequence of the fear of making mistakes), being paralyzed by doubt, immobilized, out-of-touch with impulse; avoidance of decisions and the inclination to compromise, being over-careful and cautious, prone to compulsive double checking, never being sure, lacking self-confidence, over-rehearsing, and having difficulty with unstructured situations (that is to say, those in which there is no set guideline for behavior).

If fear paralyzes or inhibits, the inhibition of impulses feeds anxiety, as was Freud's contention; and we may say that fear is a fear of one's own impulses, a fear to act spontaneously. This "fear to be," to borrow Tillich's expression, is typically complicated by a fear of the outer world and a fear of the future consequences of one's present actions. An additional way in which fear, through immobilization, re-kindles itself is through the sense of impotence that plagues an individual who dreads giving free rein to aggressive or sexual impulses. Not being able to rely on one's power, distrusting one's abilities and the capacity to cope with situations—with the consequent insecurity and the need to rely on others—may be regarded as not altogether irrational but as the result of knowing oneself to be, in a psychological sense, "castrated."

Over-alert Hyperintentionality

Closely related to anxiety but not identical to it is the hyper-alertness entailed by a suspicious and over-cautious disposition. Unlike the confident over-alertness of ennea-type III which orients itself to having "everything under control," this is a hyper-vigilance that is on the lookout for hidden meanings, clues, and the unusual. Aside from constituting a state of chronic arousal in the service of interpreting (potentially dangerous) reality, it serves an excessive deliberation concerning what for others would be a matter of spontaneous choice. I have borrowed Shapiro's word "hyper-intentionality" for the extraordinarily rigid and tense directedness of behavior (of suspicious character) as well as for the exaggerated need to rely on rational choices.

Theoretical Orientation

Fear makes the coward unable to be sure enough to act, so that he never has enough certainty and wants to know better. He not only needs guidance, but also typically (distrusting guidance as well as needing it) solves this conflict through appeal to the guidance of some logical system or of reason itself. Ennea-type VI is not only an intellectual ennea-type, but the most logical of ennea-types, one who is devoted to reason. Unlike ennea-type VII who uses intellect as strategy, ennea-type VI is likely to worship intellect through fanatical allegiance to reason and reason alone—as in scientism. In his need for answers in order to solve his problems, ennea-type VI is more than any other a questioner, and thus a potential philosopher. Not only does he use the intellect for problem-solving, but he resorts to problem *seeking* as a way to feeling safe. In his hypervigilance, his paranoid character is on the look-out for problems; he is a trouble-shooter in regard to himself and has difficulty in accepting himself without problems. While there is hope in seeing oneself with problems—the hope of being able to solve them—there is also a trap in problem-making that manifests, for instance, as an inability to go beyond the role of patient in the therapeutic process and a difficulty in just letting oneself be.

Not only is the ineffectualness or generalized problem with doing of the more timid ennea-type VI individuals a consequence of an excessive orientation to the abstract and theoretical, but seeking refuge in intellectual activity is, also, a consequence of fearful holding back, indirectness, vagueness and "beating around the bush."

Ingratiating Friendliness

Other groups of descriptors point to generalized traits understandable as ways of coping with anxiety. Thus we may understand the warmth of most ennea-type VI individuals as a weakness: a way of ingratiation. Even if we do not agree with Freud's interpretation of friendship as paranoid banding together in face of a common enemy, we must grant that there is such "friendship." The compulsive search for protection of cowardly affection falls into this category.

Together with the descriptor "affection" I list in this cluster "seeking and giving warmth," "being a good host and being hospitable," and "generous." "Pathological piety" may be also listed here, along with "exaggerated faithfulness" to individuals and causes. Also the traits of "considerateness," "gentleness," "obsequiousness," and the need for support and validation of the more insecure cowards falls in with the above. I notice that ennea-type VI individuals in whom these traits dominate are also prone to sadness, forlornness, and a sense of abandonment, much as in ennea-type IV.

Related to the ingratiating obsequiousness and the warmth of ennea-type VI is the need for association with a stronger partner, that gives them security yet typically frustrates their competitive inclinations.

Rigidity

Closely related to the affectionate expression of cowardice is an accommodating quality. The trait of obedience itself, however, I have grouped with characteristics of a more generalized dutifulness, such as an obedience to law, a devotion to fulfilling responsibilities as defined by external authority, a tendency to follow rules and to value documents and institutions. Ennea-type VI individuals in whom these traits predominate may be said to have a "Prussian character," in reference to this stereotype of rigidity and organization. The fear of authority and the fear of making mistakes causes them to need clear-cut guidelines as to what is right and wrong, so they are highly intolerant of ambiguity. These guidelines are never those of popular opinion, as in the "other directed" ennea-type III, but the rules of present or past authorities, such as the set of implicit inner rules of Don Quixote, who follows the knight errant in his imagination. Along with the above I have listed the traits "controlled," "correct," "well informed," "hard working," "punctual," "precise," and "responsible."

Pugnacity

As an alternative to both the soft, obedient, ingratiating style of coping with anxiety and the rigid, principled, rule-bound style, we find a cluster of traits that may be understood as a pugnacious intimidation through which the individual (as Freud described in connection with the oedipal struggle) competes with parental authority—and later in life uses the position of authority both to feel safe and to obtain what he wants. To the extent that competitive usurpation is involved, there is guilt, fear of retaliation, and a perpetuation of paranoid insecurity. Belonging in this category are, aside from the denouncing of authority and the competitive wish to stand in the place of authority, "argumentativeness," "criticality," "skepticism," and "cynicism."

Along with these I have listed the descriptors "they think they know the right way," "pressuring others to conform," "bombastic," "bluffing," "strong," "courageous," and "grandiose." The trait of scapegoating appears to be related to this "strong" expression of ennea-type VI rather than the warm and weak style. We are in the presence of the counter-phobic manifestation of ennea-type VI—a strategy comparable to the barking of a dog.

Orientation to Authority and Ideals

What the aggressive, the dutiful, and the affectionate safety maneuvers have in common is their relevance to authority. We may say the fear of ennea-type VI was originally aroused by parental authority and the threat of punishment by the power-wielding parent—usually the father. Just as originally his fear led to sweetness, obedience, or defiance (and usually ambivalence) toward his parents, now he continues to behave and feel the same in the face of others to whom he assigns authority or towards whom he (consciously or unconsciously) becomes one.

The pattern of "authoritarian aggression" and "authoritarian submission" noted by the authors of *The Authoritarian Personality* may be mentioned here: ennea-type VI manifests aggression towards those below and submission to those above in the authority hierarchy.[1] Not only do they live in a hierarchical world: they both hate and love authority consciously (being, in spite of anxiety in the face of ambiguity, the most explicitly ambivalent of all character ennea-types).

In addition to traits of submissiveness, the demand for obedience and love, hate and ambivalence toward authority, ennea-type VI exhibits, to a larger extent than any other, an idealization of authority figures— manifest either in individualized hero-worship, in a generalized attraction to the great and the strong or in an orientation to impersonal greatness, which causes some to over-mythologize life so as to indulge a passion for archetypal sublimity. This penchant for what is larger than life seems not only to underlie a divinization/demonization of the ordinary (observed by Jung in connection with the introverted thinking ennea-type) and the perceived sublimity of ideals of fanatics, but is a characteristic of ennea-type VI people in general, who in view of this may be described as "idealistic."

---

[1] T.W. Adorno et. al., *The Authoritarian Personality* (New York: Harper and Brothers, 1950).

Accusation of Self and Others

Guilt is as prominent in ennea-type VI character as in ennea-types IV and V, only that in ennea-type VI the mechanism of guilt production goes hand-in-hand with a prominent mechanism of exculpation through projection and the creation of outer enemies. It is not only anxiety, but guilt, we may say, that seeks to be alleviated through ingratiation, through dutiful appeasement of potential accusers, through submission to personal or intellectual authorities or through an assertive bluffing behind which the individual hides his weaknesses and imperfections. In usurpation of parental authority and becoming an authority, just as in placating authority, the individual acts not only self-protectively but blame-avoidantly.

We may say that guilt manifested in such traits as defensiveness, self-justification, and insecurity, involves an act of self-accusation by which an individual becomes an invalidating parent to himself. It is in this act of self-opposition, through which an individual becomes his or her own enemy, that I see the fixation proper of ennea-type VI, i.e., the cognitive defect that developed as a consequence of fear and has ended by becoming its root. Accusation is not only an ennea-type VI characteristic in regard to self, but also to others—perhaps through the operation of projection in the service of avoiding the torment of too much guilt. Not only does ennea-type VI persecute himself and feel persecuted, but he is a suspicious and critical persecutor—and he may affirm his grandiosity precisely in view of the entitlement that it affords to pronounce judgement on others.

Doubt and Ambivalence

To speak of self-invalidation is to speak of self-doubt, just as speaking of suspiciousness implies a doubting of others. Beyond the attitude of an accusatory inquisitor of self and other, the word "doubt" brings to mind the uncertainty of ennea-type VI in regard to his views: he both invalidates himself and he props himself up—feeling subtly as paranoid schizophrenics feel in the extreme: both persecuted and grandiose.

To say it differently: he doubts himself and he doubts his doubt; he is suspicious of others, and yet he is afraid that he may be mistaken. The result of this double perspective is, of course, chronic uncertainty in regard to choosing a course of action, and the consequent anxiety, need of support and guidance, and so on. At times—and as a defense against unbearable ambiguity—he may take before the world the position of a true believer who is absolutely sure of things. When not a fanatic, though, ennea-type VI is characterized by ambivalence, more strikingly than in any other character; and his most striking ambivalence is that of hating and loving his "authority bearing" parent at the same time.

Intellectual doubt, it seems, is only the expression of that emotional doubt in virtue of which he is torn between his hateful and his seductive selves, the wish to please and the wish to move against, to obey and to rebel, to admire and to invalidate.

3. Existential Psychodynamics

This is a particularly relevant topic in the case of ennea-type VI in view of the connection between points IX and VI in the enneagram: we may say that the fear to do entails being out-of-touch with oneself, that a lack of grounding in being translates as a fragility or weakness in regard to self-expression.

While ennea-type III is scarcely aware of its self-alienation and ennea-type IV and V dwell on it intensely, experiencing it as a sense of insubstantiality,

E.J. Gold, *Man With Moustache*,
charcoal, 10 1/2" x 15", 1987.

the experience of ontic obscuration in ennea-type VI is projected onto the future and carries a sense of fearful anticipation. It has been aptly described by R.D. Laing as the terror to look within and find that there is nobody there. There is in this situation neither an ignoring of the issue nor a meeting of it full face, but rather a not-quite-looking, a partial avoidance.

The fragility of the sense of being is also of such quality that it is suitably described by the expression which Laing proposed in connection with ontic obscuration in general: "ontic insecurity." We may say that being-loss in ennea-type VI manifests as an experience of threatened being, precarious being.[2] It is possible to think that the excessive concern of ennea-type VI with security is not rooted in physical fear or even emotional fear so much as in an excessive clutching at factors of physical and emotional security out of an insecurity that is "not of this world." Unlike the experience of the truly courageous person—the hero who can risk anything, life included, out of an implicit sense of rootedness-in-something-beyond-contingent-existence—the coward projects his ontic insecurity onto the outer layers of existence through either a generalized incapacity to risk or an excessive concern with an authority and power that serves as a guarantee for such risking.

In the case of paranoid character *sensu strictu* it is easy to understand loss of being as a derivative of a search for being—through proximity to "the great" and the nourishing of one's grandiosity—as may be illustrated by the situation of Don Quixote, who in his identification with the ideal of a knight errant of chivalry pursues a life of fancy, incompatible with the all too ordinary (non-grandiose) experience of day to day reality.

---

[2] Also Guntrip's expression "ego weakness" seems particularly appropriate for the paranoid nuance of being-loss.

In other instances it is not the grandiosity of an ideal or internalized image that becomes a being substitute, but the grandiosity of an external authority of the present or the past. In all such cases we may say that there is a confusion of being with authority and the special kind of power entailed by authority.

Just as it is true that at the psychological level proper the ennea-type VI individual gives up his *power* before authority, it is also possible to say that it is the very sense of being that is given up through its projection upon individuals, systems, or ideas endowed with a "greater than life" importance or sublimity.

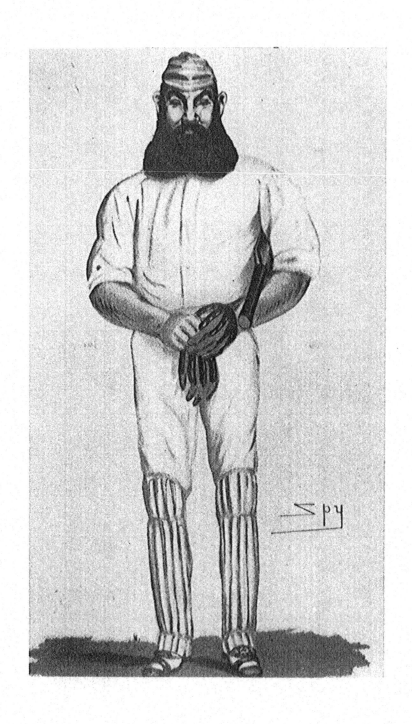

Chapter Seven

OPPORTUNISTIC IDEALISM

(Ennea-type VII)

1. Gluttony, Fraudulence and Narcissism

In the Christian world, "gluttony" is included among the seven "cardinal sins," yet its usual interpretation as a gluttony for food makes it appear somewhat less sinful than others. It would not be included among the basic sinful dispositions, however, if the original meaning of the term were not—as is the case with avarice and lust—something beyond the literal. If we understand gluttony more broadly, in the sense of a passion for pleasure, we may say that this definitely is a capital sin—inasmuch as it implies a deviation from an individual's potential for self-actualization; hedonism is binding upon the psyche and involves (through confusion) an obstacle in the search for the *summum bonum* and a snare. We may say that a weakness for pleasure constitutes a generalized susceptibility to temptation, and in this light we can understand Chaucer's statement in his "The Parson's Tale" to the effect that "He that is addicted to this sin of gluttony may withstand no other sin."[1]

---

[1] op. cit., p. 602.

When I first heard Ichazo's ideas of Protoanalysis, this was in Spanish, and he used the word "charlatan" for the ennea-type VII individual (and "charlatanism" for the fixation). This word also needs to be understood in more than a literal manner: that the glutton is one who approaches the world through the strategy of words and "good reasons"—one who manipulates through the intellect. Ichazo's later word for this personality, "ego-plan," makes reference to the fact that the "charlatan" is also a dreamer—indeed, his charlatanism may be interpreted as taking (or offering) dreams as realities. Yet I think "charlatanism" is more evocative, for planning is a prominent trait of ennea-types I and III as well, and "charlatanism" conveys additional meanings, such as expressive ability, the role of a persuader and manipulator of words, deviously overstepping the boundaries of his knowledge. More than a mere planner, ennea-type VII is a "schemer," with that strategic character that La Fontaine (a bearer of this disposition) symbolized in the fox.

Ichazo characterized gluttony as a "wanting more": I leave it up to my gluttonous readers to decide which may be the deeper interpretation. My own impression is that, though this description is characterologically apt, it points to an insatiability that gluttons share with the lusty. Also, although it is true that sometimes gluttons imagine that more of the same would bring about greater pleasure, it is also true that they more characteristically are *not* seekers of more of the same, but (romantically) seekers of the remote and the bizarre, seekers of variety, adventure, and surprise.

In the language of DSM III, the ennea-type VII syndrome receives the name of "narcissistic"—yet we must be cognizant of the fact that this is a word that has been used by different authors for other personalities as well.[2]

---

[2] For instance, most of the clinical illustrations in Lowen's book on narcissism correspond to our ennea-type III.

2. Trait Structure

Gluttony

Ennea-type VII individuals are more than just open minded, exploratory: their search for experience takes them, characteristically, from an insufficient here to a promising there. The insatiability of the glutton is, however, veiled over by an apparent satisfaction; or more precisely said, frustration is hidden behind enthusiasm—an enthusiasm that seems to compensate for dissatisfaction as well as keeping the experience of frustration away from the individual's awareness.

Whether in the question of food or in other realms, the gluttony of the glutton is typically not for the common, but, on the contrary, for that which is most remarkable, for the extraordinary. In line with this is the characteristic interest in what is magical or esoteric itself, a manifestation of a broader interest in what is remote—either geographically, culturally, or at the fringes of knowledge.

Also, an attraction to that which is beyond the boundaries of one's own culture reflects the same displacement of values from here to there; and the same may be said of the typical anti-conventional tendencies of ennea-type VII. In this case, the ideal may be in a utopian, futuristic, or progressive outlook rather than in existing cultural models.

Hedonistic Permissiveness

A pair of traits inseparable from the gluttonous pleasure bias are the avoidance of suffering and, concomitantly, the hedonistic orientation, characteristic of ennea-type VII personality. Intrinsically connected to these traits are permissiveness and self-indulgence. In connection with permissiveness it may be said that it

not only describes a trait of the individual with regard to himself, but a characteristic *laissez-faire* attitude toward others; such permissiveness sometimes even becomes complicity when gluttons seductively become friends of other people's vices.

Closely related to self-indulgence is the trait of being "spoiled," usually employed in reference to an attitude of entitlement to gratification. Also the "playboy" orientation to life falls in here and, indirectly, the exaggerated sense of okayness that the individual develops as a protection of hedonism against pain and frustration: the "optimistic attitude" that not only makes him and others OK, but the whole world a good one to live in. In some cases we may speak of a "cosmic okayness," in which the individual's contentedness is supported by a view of the world in which there is no good or evil, no guilt, no shoulds, no duties and no need to make any efforts—for it is enough to enjoy.

Rebelliousness

Of course, without rebelliousness self-indulgence would not be possible in the inhibiting world of present civilization. The main things to be said of ennea-type VII rebellion are that it manifests most visibly in a keen eye for conventional prejudices and that it usually finds a humorous outlet. Also, the rebelliousness is mostly embodied in an anti-conventional orientation while intellectual rebellion goes hand-in-hand with a good measure of behavioral acquiescence. This characteristic makes ennea-type VII people the ideologists of revolutions, rather than the activists.

Ennea-type VII is typically *not* oriented towards authorities. It might be said that the glutton has "learned" early in life that there is no good authority, yet adopts toward authority an attitude that is diplomatic rather than oppositional. An aspect of implicit rebellion is the fact that the ennea-type VII

individual mostly lives in a non-hierarchal psychological environment: just as ennea-type VI perceives
himself exaggeratedly in terms of his relationships to
superiors and inferiors, ennea-type VII is "equalitarian"
in her approach to people. Neither does she take
authority too seriously (for this would militate against
her self-indulgence, permissiveness, lack of guilt, and
superiority) nor does she present to others as an
authority, except in a covert way which seeks to
impress while at the same time assuming the garb of
modesty.

Lack of Discipline

Still another trait that is both independent enough
to be considered as such and yet dynamically dependent on gluttony and rebellion, manifests through the
lack of discipline, instability, lack of commitment, and
the dilettantish features of ennea-type VII. The word
"play-boy" reflects not only hedonism but the non-
committed attitude of an enjoyer. The lack of discipline
in this character is a consequence of his interest in not
postponing pleasure—and, at a deeper level, rests on
the perception of pleasure-postponement as lovelessness.

Imaginary Wish Fulfillment

The cathexis of fantasy and orientation to plans and
utopia are part of the gluttonous bias that, like a child at
the nipple, clings to an all too sweet and non-frustrating
world. Closely related to the above and also an escape
from the harsh realities of life is the attraction towards
the future and the potential: gluttons usually have a
futuristic orientation for through an identification with
plans and ideals, the individual seems to live
imaginatively in them rather than in down-to-earth
reality.

Seductively Pleasing

There are two facets in the ennea-type VII personality, each of which has given rise to the popular recognition of the character ("happy" and "amiable" respectively) and which together contribute to the characteristically pleasing quality of ennea-type VII character. Just as ennea-type VII is a glutton for what is pleasant and has come to feel loved through the experience of pleasure—he seems bent on fulfilling the pleasure-gluttony of those he wants to seduce. Like ennea-type II on the antipodes of the enneagram, ennea-type VII is eminently seductive, and is bent on pleasing through both helpfulness and a problem-free, cheerful contentedness. The amiable aspect of this character is alluded to by such descriptors as "warm," "helpful," "friendly," "obliging," "selflessly ready to serve" and "generous." Gluttons are very good hosts and can be great spenders. In the degree to which generosity is a part of seductiveness and a way of buying love rather than a true giving, it is counterbalanced in the psyche of the glutton by its corresponding opposite: a hidden but effective exploitativeness that may manifest as a parasitic tendency and perhaps in feelings of entitlement to care and affection.

The state of satisfied well-being of ennea-type VII rests partly on the priorities of an enjoyer, partly on the glutton's knack for imaginary fulfillment. Yet, "feeling good" also serves the ends of seductiveness and seductive motivation may at times make ennea-type VII specially cheerful, humorous, and entertaining. The good humor of ennea-type VII makes other people feel lighted-up in their presence, and this contributes effectively to the pleasure they cause and the attractiveness of being near to them, to the extent that happiness is, at least in part, seductive and definitely compulsive. The happy bias of ennea-type VII (as in the case of ennea-type III) is maintained at the expense of the repression and avoidance of pain, and results in an impoverishment of experience. In particular the "cool" of ennea-type VII involves a repression of such anxiety as chronically feeds the attitude of taking refuge in pleasure.

Narcissism

Another group of traits that may be discerned as an expression of seduction may be called narcissistic. It comprises such descriptors as "exhibitionist," "knows better," "well-informed," "intellectually superior." Sometimes this manifests as a compulsion to explain things, such as Fellini seeks to portray in movies where a narrator constantly puts into words everything that is taking place.

We may speak of a "seduction through superiority" which most usually takes the form of intellectual superiority, though (as in Molière's Tartuffe) it may involve a religious, good and saintly image. The apparent lack of grandiosity in such saintly image is sometimes manifest even in the case of those who actively seek to assert their superiority, wisdom, and kindness. This falls in line with the fact that gluttons tend to form equalitarian brotherly relationships rather than authority relations. Because of this, their pre-tended superiority is implicit rather than explicit, masked over by a non-assuming, appreciative, and equalitarian style. As in the case of pleasingness, the superiority of ennea-type VII expresses only half of the glutton's experience; the other is the simultaneous perception of self as inferior, and the corresponding feelings of insecurity. As in ennea-type V, splitting allows the simultaneity of the two sub-selves, yet while it is the deprecated self that is in the foreground in ennea-type V, it is the grandiose self that has the upper hand in the narcissistic personality.

A psychological characteristic that is important to mention in connection with the gratified narcissism of the "oral-receptive" is charm, a quality into which converge the admirable qualities of ennea-type VII (giftedness, perceptiveness, wit, savoir-vivre, and so on) and its pleasing, non-aggressive, vaseline-like, cool and contented characteristics. Through charm the glutton can satisfy his gluttony as effectively as a fisherman succeeds with bait, which implies that pleasing and charm are not just seductive but manipulative. Through his great charm the glutton can enchant others and even himself. Among his skills is that of fascination—hypnotic fascination even—and charm is his magic.

Along with the narcissistic facet of ennea-type VII it is necessary to mention the high intuition and frequent talents of ennea-type VII, which suggests that such dispositions may have favored the development of their dominant strategy (just as the adoption of the strategy has stimulated their development).

Persuasiveness

We may think of ennea-type VII as a person in whom love seeking has turned to pleasure seeking and who in the necessary measure of rebellion that this entails, sets out to satisfy his wishes through becoming a skillful explainer and rationalizer. A charlatan is of course one who is able to persuade others of the usefulness of what he sells. However, beyond the intellectual activity of explanation, which can become a narcissistic vice in ennea-type VII, persuasiveness rests in one's own belief in one's wisdom, superiority, respectability and goodness of intentions. Thus only artificially can we separate traits that exist in close inter-wovenness: being admirable serves persuasiveness, as also does pleasingness.

The qualities of being a persuader and a knowledge source usually find expression in ennea-type VII in

becoming an adviser at times in a professional capacity.
Charlatans like to influence others through advice. We
may see not only narcissistic satisfaction and the expression of helpfulness in charlatanism but an interest in
manipulating through words: "laying trips" on people
and having them implement the persuader's projects.
Along with a manipulative motivation to influence
others we may consider the high intelligence, high
verbal ability, capability of suggesting, and so forth, that
usually characterize ennea-type VII individuals.

Fraudulence

We have discussed the polarity of feeling OK (and
better than OK) and of being at the same time driven by
an oral passion to suck at the best of life. We have
spoken of a rebelliousness as described in Fritz Perls'
observation that "behind every good boy one may find
a spiteful brat." We have encountered in ennea-type VII
a confusion between imagination and reality, between
projects and accomplishments, potentialities and rea-
lizations. Then, we have encountered a pleasingness, a
persona-hiding anxiety, a smoothness hiding aggression, a generosity hiding exploitativeness. The word
"charlatan" of ennea-type VII in its connotation of fake
knowledge and confusion between verbal map and
territory has thus an appropriateness to the character
beyond mere persuasiveness. Taken broadly, it conveys
a more generalized fraudulence (to which all the above
add up). Indeed the conceptual label "fraudulence" may
be more appropriate than the symbolic or metaphoric
"charlatanism" for the ennea-type's fixation.

3. Existential Psychodynamics

It remains to elaborate how, as in other character ennea-types, the ruling passion is supported, day after day, not just through memories of past gratification and frustration, but through the interference that that character entails on healthy function and self-realization.

As in the case of the other passions, we may understand gluttony as an attempt to fill an emptiness. Gluttony, just as oral-aggressive envy, seeks outside what it dimly perceives as lacking inside: only that unlike envy (in which there is pronounced awareness of ontic insufficiency) gluttony fraudulently covers up the insufficiency with a false abundance comparable to that of pride. (In this way the passion is acted out without full self-awareness.)

Ontic deficiency is not only the source of hedonism (and pain avoidance) however, but also its consequence; for the confusion between love and pleasure fails to bring about the deeper meaningfulness than that of the immediately available. A sense of inner scarcity is also, of course, supported by alienation of the individual from his experiential depth, which occurs as a consequence of the hedonistic need to experience only what is pleasing. It is nurtured also by the implicit fear that permeates the ennea-type in its soft accommodatingness—a fear not compatible with the living of one's true life. It is also supported by manipulativeness, which, just as in ennea-type VIII, presupposes loss of true relationship (however masked by amiability this may be), a divorcing of oneself from the sense of community (however masked this may be in ennea-type VII) by the fraudulent sense of community that is part of seductive charm.

Finally the orientation of gluttony to the spiritual, the esoteric and the paranormal, while seeking to

E.J. Gold, *Jazzman,*
pen and ink, 11" x 15", 1968.

constitute the exact answer for the ontic deficiency that lies at its core, only serves to perpetuate it—for, by seeking being in the future, in the remote, the imagined, and the beyond, the individual only assures his frustration in finding value in the present and the actual.

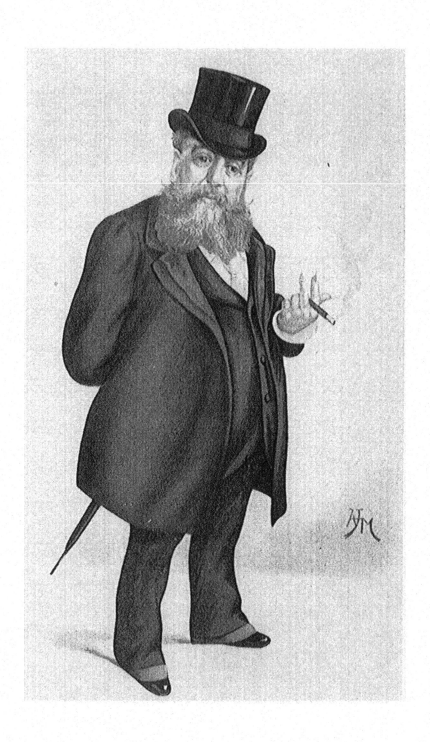

Chapter Eight

COMING ON STRONG

(Ennea-type VIII)

1. Lust and Vindictive Arrogance

The Spanish dictionary from the Spanish Royal Academy—where I dictate this chapter—says concerning lust that it is a "vice consisting in the illicit use or disordered appetite for carnal pleasures," and gives the additional meaning of "excess in certain things."

It is the latter definition which coincides with the meaning given to the term by Ichazo in his exposition of Protoanalysis, and we may view the former, i.e. the more common sense of the term, as its derivative or corollary. I will therefore use the word "lust" to denote a passion for excess, a passion that seeks intensity, not only through sex, but in all manner of stimulation: activity, anxiety, spices, high speed, the pleasure of loud music, and so on.

Lust is mapped in the enneagram next to the upper vertex of the inner triangle, which indicates its kinship to indolence, to a sensory-motor disposition and the predominance of cognitive obscuration or "ignorance" over "aversion" and "craving" (at the left and right corners, respectively). The indolent aspect of the lusty may be understood not only as a feeling of not-alive-enough-except-through-over-stimulation but also in a concomitant avoidance of inwardness. We may say that

the greed for ever more aliveness, characteristic of the
lusty personality, is but an attempt to compensate for a
hidden lack of aliveness.

Opposite to envy on the enneagram, lust may be
said to constitute the upper pole of a sado-masochistic
axis. The two personalities, VIII and IV, are in some way
opposite (as these terms suggest), though also similar in
some regards, such as in the thirst for intensity. Also,
just as a masochistic character is in some ways sadistic,
there is a masochistic aspect in the character of lust; and
while a sadistic character is active, a masochistic disposition is emotional: the former reaches out without
guilt towards the satisfaction of its need; the latter
yearns and feels guilty about its neediness.

Just as the envy-centered character is the most
sensitive in the enneagram, ennea-type VIII is the most
*in*sensitive. We may envision the passion for intensity
of ennea-type VIII as an attempt to seek through action
the intensity that ennea-type IV achieves through
emotional sensitivity, which here is not only veiled over
by the basic indolence that this ennea-type shares with
the upper triad of the enneagram but also by a
desensitization in the service of counter-dependent
self-sufficiency.

The characterological syndrome of lust is related to
that of gluttony in that both are characterized by
impulsiveness and hedonism. In the case of gluttony,
however, impulsiveness and hedonism exist in the
context of a weak, soft and tender-minded characterological context, while in lust the context is that of a
strong and tough-minded character.[1]

The anti-social personality disorder described in
DSM III may be regarded as a pathological extreme and

---

[1] The connection between gluttony and lust has been observed long
ago, it seems, for we may read in Chaucer's, "The Parson's Tale" (op.
cit.): "After gluttony, then comes lechery; for these two sins are such
close cousins that oftentimes they will not be separated."

a special instance of ennea-type VIII. The broader syndrome may be better evoked through Reich's label of "phallic narcissistic" character or Horney's description of the vindictive personality. The word "sadistic" seems particularly appropriate in view of its position opposite the masochistic character of ennea-type IV.

2. Trait Structure

Lust

Just as anger may be regarded as the most hidden of passions, lust is probably the most visible, seeming an exception to a general rule that wherever there is passion, there is also taboo or injunction in the psyche against it. I say "seemingly" because even though the lusty ennea-type is passionately in favor of his lust and of lust in general as a way of life, the very passionateness with which he embraces this outlook betrays a defensiveness—as if he needed to prove to himself and the rest of the world that what everybody calls bad is not such. Some of the specific traits that convey lust such as "intensity," "gusto," "contactfulness," "love of eating," and so on, are intimately bound to the constitutional stratum of personality. A sensory-motor disposition (the somatotonic background of lust) may be regarded as the natural soil in which lust proper is supported. Other traits, such as hedonism, the propensity to boredom when not sufficiently stimulated, the craving for excitement, impatience, and impulsiveness, are in the domain of lust proper.

We must consider that lust is more than hedonism. There is in lust not only pleasure, but pleasure in asserting the satisfaction of impulses, pleasure in the forbidden and, particularly, pleasure in *fighting for pleasure*. In addition to pleasure proper there is here an admixture of some pain that has been transformed into

pleasure: either the pain of others who are "preyed upon" for one's satisfaction or the pain entailed by the effort to conquer the obstacles in the way to satisfaction. It is this that makes lust a passion for intensity and not for pleasure alone. The extra intensity, the extra excitement, the "spice," comes not from instinctual satisfaction, but from a struggle and an implicit *triumph*.

Punitiveness

Another group of traits intimately connected to lust is that which could be labeled punitive, sadistic, exploitative, hostile. Among such traits we can find "bluntness," "sarcasm," "irony" and those of being intimidating, humiliating, and frustrating. Of all characters, this is the most angry and the least intimidated by anger.

It is the angry and punitive characteristic of ennea-type VIII Ichazo addresses in his calling the fixation of the lusty "revenge." The word, however, has the drawback of being associated with the most overtly vindictive of the characters, ennea-type IV, whose hatefulness sometimes manifests in explicit *vendettas*. In this overt sense ennea-type VIII is not strikingly vindictive; on the contrary, the character retaliates angrily at the moment and gets quickly over his irritation. The revenge which is most present in ennea-type VIII is (aside from "getting even" in the immediate response) a long-term one, in which the individual takes justice in his own hands in response to the pain, humiliation, and impotence felt in early childhood. It is as if he wanted to turn the tables on the world and, after having suffered frustration or humiliation for the pleasure of others, has determined that it is now his turn to have pleasure even if it involves the pain of others. Or *especially* then—for in this, too, may lie revenge.

The sadistic phenomenon of enjoying the frustration or humiliation of others may be regarded as a transformation of having to live with one's own (as a byproduct of vindictive triumph), just as the *excitement* of anxiety, strong tastes, and tough experiences represents a transformation of pain in the process of hardening oneself against life.

The anti-social characteristic of ennea-type VIII, like rebellion itself (in which it is embedded), may be regarded as a reaction of anger at the world and thus a manifestation of vindictive punitiveness. The same may be said of dominance, insensitivity and cynicism, along with their derivatives. Punitiveness can be regarded as the fixation in sadistic or exploitative character—and we may credit Horney and Fromm for being ahead of their time in stressing these last-mentioned characteristics.

Rebelliousness

Though lust itself implies an element of rebellion in its assertive opposition to the inhibition of pleasure, rebellion stands out as a trait on its own, more prominent in ennea-type VIII than in any other character. Even though ennea-type VII is unconventional, the emphasis of this rebellion is intellectual. He is a person with "advanced ideas," perhaps a revolutionary outlook, while ennea-type VIII is the prototype of the revolutionary activist. Beyond specific ideologies, however, there is in the character not only a strong opposition to authority, but a scorn for the values enjoined by traditional education. It is in virtue of such blunt invalidation of authority, that "badness" automatically becomes the way to be. Generalized rebellion against authority can usually be traced back to a rebellion in the face of the father, who is the carrier of authority in the family. Vindictive characters frequently learn not to expect anything good from their fathers and implicitly come to regard parental power as illegitimate.

Dominance

Closely related to the characteristic hostility of the ennea-type is dominance. Hostility may be said to be in the service of dominance, and dominance, in turn, regarded as an expression of hostility. Yet, dominance also serves the function of protecting the individual from a position of vulnerability and dependency. Related to dominance are such traits as "arrogance," "power seeking," "need for triumph," "putting others down," "competitiveness," "acting superior," and so on. Also related to these traits of superiority and dominance are the corresponding traits of disdain and scorn for others. It is easy to see how dominance and aggressiveness are in the service of lust; particularly in a world that expects individual restraint, only power and the ability to fight for one's wishes can allow the individual to indulge in his passion for impulse expression. Dominance and hostility stand in service of vindictiveness, as if the individual had early in life decided that it doesn't pay to be weak, accommodating, or seductive, and has oriented himself toward power in an attempt to take justice in his own hands.

Insensitivity

Also closely related to the hostile characteristic of ennea-type VIII are traits of toughness, manifest through such descriptors as "confrontativeness," "intimidation," "ruthlessness," "callousness." Such characteristics are clearly a consequence of an aggressive style of life, not compatible with fear or weakness, sentimentality or pity. Related to this unsentimental, realistic, direct, brusque, blunt quality, there is a corresponding disdain for the opposite qualities of weakness, sensitivity and, particularly, fear. We may say that a specific instance of the toughening of the psyche is an exaggerated risk-taking characteristic, through which the individual denies his own fears and indulges the feeling of power generated by his internal conquest. Risk-taking, in turn, feeds lust, for the ennea-type VIII individual has learned to thrive on anxiety as a source of excitement, and rather than *suffering*, he has—through an implicit masochistic phenomenon—learned to wallow in its sheer intensity. Just as his palate has learned to interpret the painful sensations of a hot spice as pleasure, anxiety—and/or the process of hardening oneself against it—has become, more than a pleasure, a psychological addiction, something without which life seems tasteless and boring.

Conning and Cynicism

The next two traits can be considered intimately connected. The cynical attitude to life of the exploitative personality is underscored by Fromm's traits of skepticism, the tendency to look upon virtue as always hypocritical, distrust in the motives of others, and so on. In these traits, as in toughness, we see the expression of a way and a vision of life, "red in tooth and claw."[2]

In regard to conning and cunning, it should be said that ennea-type VIII is more blatantly deceptive than ennea-type VII, and is easily seen as a cheat, the typical "used car salesman" who knows how to bargain assertively.

Exhibitionism (Narcissism)

Ennea-type VIII people are entertaining, witty, and often charming, yet not vain in the sense of being concerned with how they appear. Their seductiveness, bragging, and arrogant claims are consciously manipulative; they are geared to gaining influence and

---

[2] Fromm, Erich, *Man For Himself: An Inquiry into the Psychology of Ethics* (New York: Holt, Rinehart and Winston, 1964).

elevation in the power and dominance hierarchy. They also constitute a compensation for exploitativeness and insensitivity, a way of buying out others or making themselves acceptable despite traits of unaccountability, violence, invasiveness, and so on.

Autonomy

As Horney has remarked, we could not expect anything other than self-reliance in one who approaches others as potential competitors or targets of exploitation. Along with the characteristic autonomy of ennea-type VIII is the *idealization* of autonomy, a corresponding rejection of dependency and passive oral strivings. The rejection of these passive traits is so striking that Reich postulated that phallic-narcissistic character constitutes precisely a defense against them.[3]

Sensorimotor Dominance

Beyond the concepts of lust and hedonism, rebellion, punitiveness, dominance and power-seeking, toughness, risk-taking, narcissism, astuteness, is in ennea-type VIII the predominance of action over intellect and feeling, for this is the most sensory-motor of characters. The characteristic orientation of ennea-type VIII to a graspable and concrete "here and now"—the sphere of the senses and the body-sense in particular—is a lusty clutching at the present and an excited impatience toward memory, abstractions, anticipations, as well as a desensitization to the subtlety of aesthetic and spiritual experience. Concentration on the present is not simply a manifestation of mental health as it could be in other character dispositions, but the consequence of not deeming anything real that is not tangible and an immediate stimulus to the senses.

[3] Reich, Wilhelm, *Character Analysis*, translated by Vincent Carfagno (New York: Simon and Schuster, 1972).

Léger

Eugene Gold 7/21/52

E.J. Gold, F. *Leger, the Workers' Hero,*
pen and ink, 11" x 15", 1952.

3. Existential Psychodynamics

The over-development of action in the service of struggling in a dangerous world that cannot be trusted is perhaps the fundamental way in which ennea-type VIII character fails to constitute full humanness. To elucidate further its existential interpretation we need to understand the vicious circle by which not only ontic obscuration supports lust, but lust, in its impetuous grasping at the tangible, entails an impoverishment of tender qualities and subtlety which results in a loss of wholeness and thus in a loss of being. It is as if the lusty character, in his impatience for satisfaction, shifts to an excessively concrete notion of his goal as pleasure, wealth, triumph, and so forth—only to find that this reaching, substituted for being, leaves him forever dissatisfied, craving intensity.

The situation may be explained through the paradigm of the rapist—an extrapolation of the lusty predator's approach to life. He has given up the expectation of being wanted, to say nothing of love. He takes for granted that he will only get what he takes. As a taker, he could not succeed if he were to be concerned with the fancy of other people's feelings. The way to be a winner is clear: to put winning before all else; likewise, the way to having one's needs met is to forget the other. The world without others of the more anti-social ennea-type VIII, however, is no more full of true aliveness than that of the schizoid ennea-type V. Just as the schizoid misses the experience of value and being through the loss of relationship, so does the psychopath, in spite of seeming to be contactful, involved, and brimming with intense emotion.

The paradigm of rape can also serve as a background to a further discussion of the semblance of being which the sadistic ennea-type fails to know that he is pursuing. The concreteness of a wish that is excessively sensate (here an interest in sexual pleasure not coupled with an interest in relationship) is an image through which we may reflect on how the concretization of the healthy drive for relationship, far from orienting itself to the reality of the situation (as "realistic phallic-narcissists" claim), involves a blatant lack of psychological reality. The situation conveys a sexualization of lust-centered personality as a result of the repression, denial, and transformation of the need for love.

Hidden as it may be behind the enthusiastic expansiveness, jollity, and seductive charm of the lusty, it is the loss of relationship, the suppression of tenderness, and the denial of the love need that result in the loss of wholeness and sense of being.

Ennea-type VIII pursues being, then, in pleasure and in the power to find his pleasure, yet through an insistence on overpowering becomes incapable of receiving—when being can only be known in a receptive attitude. By doggedly claiming satisfaction where a *semblance* of satisfaction can be imagined, much as Nasruddin seeks his key in the market place, he perpetuates an ontic deficiency that only feeds his lusty pursuit of triumph and other being substitutes.

Chapter Nine

"GOING WITH THE STREAM"

(Ennea-type IX)

1. Accidia, the Passion for Comfort and the Over-Adjusted Disposition

The words "laziness" and "indolence" with which Ichazo designated the ruling passion and the fixation (respectively) corresponding to ennea-type IX, fail to convey what they were originally intended to signify— before "sloth" was introduced instead of the earlier Latin term *accidia*.

Professor Giannini, of the University of Chile, writes, "What Saint Thomas, Gregory the Great, Saint Isidore, Cassian (to cite only the more representative authors) designated as *accidia* is a very complex phenomenon and far from translations such as lack of motivation toward action and other contemporary translations."[1]

In turn, a translation from the Greek *a-chedia* (no care), *accidia* refers to a laziness of the psyche and of the spirit, rather than a tendency to inaction, and so does "indolence" in the context of this book. Such spiritual laziness may be spoken of in terms of a forgetfulness of God or, in non-theistic language, a deafening to the

---

[1] H. Giannini: "El demonio del Mediodia," In *Teoria*, Dic. 1975, Santiago de Chile.

spirit and a loss of the sense of being to the point of not
even knowing the difference—a spiritual coarsening.
Psychologically, *accidia* manifests as a loss of interiority,
a refusal to see, and a resistance to change.

The combination of loss of interiority and the
resigned and abnegated character that goes along with
it, results in a syndrome of a good-hearted, comfortable
"earthiness" that may be exaggerated to the point of
literalness and narrowness.

Ennea-type IX is not only one that has not learned
to love him- or herself as a consequence of love
deprivation, but one who forgets his love frustration
through a sort of psychological pachydermism, an over-
simplification, a psychological amputation that makes
him the least sensitive and the most stoic of characters.
(Ennea-type IX stands opposite to the hyper-sensitives
IV and V at the bottom of the enneagram.)

No less important than the etymology of the word is
what Saint Thomas writes of it when he tells us that
accidia is "sadness that makes us slow in spiritual
deeds."[2] Not only is a laziness in regard to spiritual
deeds addressed, but it is suggested that this is an
attitude sustained by a depressive emotional context.

Precise as all the above may be, it fails to suggest the
pervasiveness of spiritual laziness in the world, and its
manifestations outside of hermitages and monasteries.
For it is not a lack of religiosity that characterizes
ennea-type IX but rather the contrary—only that this
tends to be a religiosity in the social and ideological
implications of the word rather than in reference to its
mystical core. Ennea-type IX is, as we shall see, the
contented and generous type of person whose "sloth"
reveals itself not so much in an aversion to spiritual
things as in a loss of inwardness, an aversion to
psychological exploration, and with a resistance to
change that exists side by side with an excessive

---

[2] Thomas Aquinas, *Summa Theologia* (S.S. 935 art 3C, Barcelona:
BAC).

stability and a conservative inclination. His motto—to himself and others—could be "don't rock the boat."

2.Trait Structure

Psychological Inertia

When I seek to bring order into the list of ennea-type IX descriptors through classification according to felt psychological commonality, I find that one of the conceptual clusters implies a trait that could be understood as a "paucity of inner experiences," to use Horney's expression in a paper by the same title, a lack of fire, a phlegmatic lack of passion. Along with these terms we may link "narcotization" (also introduced by Horney) and "thick-skinned" (a desensitization in the service of "long suffering"). An intellectual expression of the defensive loss of inwardness is a lack of subtlety and of imagination; an emotional consequence, a deadening of feelings, which may be either apparent (in an excessively phlegmatic disposition or in lack of communication about self) or hidden (under a genial or jovial disposition).

At the cognitive level, the most decisive aspect of it is the person's deafening to his or her inner voices—a loss of instinct well hidden by an apparent animalization (just as a pseudo-spontaneity of sexual and social freedom coexists with an inner deadening).

Not wanting to see, not wanting to be in touch with one's experience, is something akin to cognitive laziness, an eclipse of the experiencer or inner witnessing in the person. In line with such eclipse of cognition in the light of a predominantly active disposition is a trait that may be called "concretism," the expression of which ranges from literalness to an excessively earthbound attitude, a Sancho-Panzaesque concern for survival and practicality at the expense of the subtle

and the mysterious—a loss of openness to the unexpected and to the spirit.

Over-Adaptation

If spiritual laziness or *accidia* is the passion in ennea-type IX, the interpersonal life strategy and associated life view may be seen in a cluster having to do with "over-adaptation," "self-denial," "self-neglect," "inattention to personal needs," and "an over-controlled disposition"—which I am including in the same group—for it is not possible to adjust (to say nothing of over-adjusting) without the ability to take hold of oneself and inhibit one's impulses. It is against the background of this disciplined and controlled aspect of ennea-type IX (a trait that it shares with ennea-type I with somewhat less intensity) that we can understand the alcoholic propensity of this character as well as the passion for eating. Both illustrate a compensatory indulgence of physical appetites that does not constitute an intensification of aliveness.

Other descriptors corresponding here are "deliberate" and "responsible." An ennea-type IX individual is not only one who ends up "carrying the bucket," but a dependable as well as generous person ready to carry a large load over his or her shoulders. If in most cases the failure to embody the ideal of loving one's neighbor as oneself comes from loving oneself more than one's neighbor, in ennea-type IX, the situation appears as the opposite, for the over-adjusted postpone their own good and the satisfaction of their needs in an excessive yieldingness to the demands and needs of others.

It is easy to understand the connection between the two above-described traits: excessive adaptation to the world would be too painful to endure without self-forgetfulness.

Resignation

Both self-alienation and abnegated over-adaptation involve resignation—a giving up of oneself, an abdication from oneself and from life. It is as if the individual endorsed a strategy of playing dead to stay alive (yet becoming tragically dead-in-life in the name of life). Though resignation underlies over-adaptation, it deserves to be considered by itself in view of the prominence of traits involving laziness in regard to one's needs, contentedness, and giving up or not standing up for one's rights.

Generosity

Related to a predominant orientation towards adaptation, in addition to a generalized "goodness of nature," "kindness," "helpfulness," "forgivingness," and above all "abnegation," may be considered the "heartiness" of ennea-type IX, the friendly conviviality and the extroverted jollity of the "cyclothymic." It would seem that such jollity is part of an attitude of taking oneself lightly in order not to weigh upon others, just as friendliness is supported by the ability to be for the other more than for oneself. The convivial and hypomaniac aspect of the "viscerotonic" was well known to Dickens, who gave us a wonderful portrayal of it in Mr. Micawber in *David Copperfield*. The over-adjusted individual characteristically likes children, is fond of animals, enjoys gardening. In his relation to others he is usually a good listener, ready to be helpful, sympathetic, and comforting, perhaps commiserating.

Ordinariness

Ennea-type IX individuals are frequently described as unassuming. Their self-concept is likely to be low—which often involves a resignation in terms of narcissistic needs. Their concern about excelling or shining is also low, and they may neglect their personal appearance. A characteristic ordinarity, a plainness and simplicity seem to derive from the giving up of the concern to excel and shine. (Ennea-type IX wants neither to shine, like ennea-type III, nor to be the best as ennea-type I). Though individuals with this character seem to have given up the wish for recognition, there is a deep and unconscious love thirst in their abnegated resignation and an implicit wish for love retribution. The sense of worth as well as the sense of existence of ennea-type IX is satisfied, not through applause, but rather, through vicarious participation, a living through others: lost identity becomes an identity by symbiosis with family, nation, party, club, team, and so on. We might speak of interiority through participation, either at the sentimental, the familial, or the larger group level.

Robotic Habit-Boundedness

Different traits emerging from the clustering of descriptors have to do with being "robotic." The over-adjusted are creatures of habit. They are bound by custom and regularity, as Sheldon observes of viscero-tonics in general. They are excessively concerned with the preservation of their balance. As a corollary, they tend to be conservative and tradition-directed to the point of rigidity. The same trait of psychological inertia may be thought to underlie an excessive attachment to the familiar, to the group norms or "how things are done."[1] Robotization, of course, can be seen as a consequence of loss of interiority, of alienation from self. On the whole we are struck by the paradox that this most painstaking and long suffering way of being

1) Also, and perhaps as a compensation—in view of their over-adaptiveness—they are characteristically hard-headed and stubborn, in a narrow-minded and prejudiced manner that they also share with ennea-type I.

in the world is rooted in a passion for comfort: a psychological comfort purchased at such high price that, as intimated above, bioenergetics practitioners brand ennea-type IX individuals as "masochistic."

Distractibility

From what has been said it is clear that ennea-type IX approaches life through a strategy of not wanting to see, and this results in an over-simplification of the outer and inner world, a diminished capacity for psychological insight and also an intellectual laziness: a simpleton quality, characterized by excessive concreteness and literalness. It is not surprising that a loss of inwardness and insight entail a spiritual consequence— a loss of the subtlety of awareness required to sustain the sense of being beyond the manyfold experiences in the sensory-motor domain.

That a perturbation of consciousness is involved in these various obscurations seems confirmed in the fact that ennea-type IX people describe themselves as distractible, confused, sometimes with a bad memory. It seems to me that it is common for ennea-type IX to break things or have personal accidents, and I think this observation may be the basis for the statistical fact of a correlation between death by car accidents and obesity. The nature of their attention problem seems to be a difficulty of concentration—which causes awareness to escape from the center of the experience realm toward its periphery. This distractibility of attention is assisted, however, by the individual's deliberate pursuit of distractions, as if driven by the desire not to experience or not to see. TV, newspapers, sewing, cross-word puzzles, and activity in general—in addition to sleep—serve the purpose of narcotization or "numbing out."

3. Existential Psychodynamics

Just as at the bottom of the enneagram (IV and V) conscious existential pain is maximal, in ennea-type IX, at the top, it is minimal; and while ontic obscuration in ennea-type III is better intuited by an outsider who may ask "what is all the rush about?" than by the subject himself, in ennea-type IX not even an outsider would guess the loss of inwardness on the individual's part, for his contentedness seems to radiate in such a way that he seems more *there* to others than he himself feels. Precisely in this lies the special characteristic of the ontic obscuration in the indolent, over-adjusted disposition—that it has become blind to itself.

Throughout the elucidation of the loss-of-being in other characters we have noted how a craving for being, in its impatience, seems to fix itself upon different appearances where there lies an ontic promise. In the case of ennea-type IX, rather, it is not the intensification of "ontic libido" that stands in the foreground but, on the contrary, a seeming lack of craving that gives the person an aura of spiritual fulfillment.

Yet the seeming enlightenment of the "healthy peasant" entails an unconsciousness of unconsciousness, a falling asleep to his yearning. I cannot understand Ichazo's statement to the effect that in indolence "the trap" is being too much of a seeker. Characteristically, the opposite is true: ennea-type IX is not enough of a seeker, despite the subjective sense of being so and despite manifestations of displaced seeking such as erudition, travelling, or collecting antiquities. Indeed such negative transmutation of the transformative urge into impulses oriented toward a less dimensioned venture is typical, and may express itself in a desire to know curiosities. Dickens' Mr. Pickwick is a good literary example in his venturing

E.J. Gold, *The Sculptor*,
pastel, 9" x 12", 1986.

beyond the outskirts of London, learning languages, and so on.

As I have examined the existential psycho-dynamics of the different characters thus far, I have been spelling out the contention—expressed by the central position of ennea-type IX in the enneagram of characters—that the "forgetting of self" is the root of all pathologies. While in other instances this transpersonal perturbation seems the background for striking interpersonal consequences, in ennea-type IX it is the foreground, and a relative paucity of compensatory consequences gives the impression of interpersonal health, "pseudo maturity." We may say that ennea-type IX is less neurotic than other characters in the ordinary sense of the word that makes reference to psychological symptoms proper, and that its perturbation is more purely spiritual.

Even though the being-substitutes of ennea-type IX are not in the foreground—as in the frantic speeded-up psychology of vanity or in the intensity search of the masochistic or the sadistic personalities—this "search for being in the wrong place" is there, as it is in all characters. One of its forms I have called "over-creaturization": a search for being in the realm of creature comforts and survival-related practicalities. Such a person might say, "I eat therefore I am." Another form is the pursuit of being through belonging. For the ennea-type IX individual, the needs of others are his own needs and their joys are his joys. Living symbiotically, he lives vicariously. He could say, "I am you, therefore I exist"—where the "you" can be a loved one, a nation, a political party, a Pickwickian club, even a football team....

Though compulsive abnegation develops in part as a response to the belonging drive, it also serves as a function of ontic compensation: "I am because I can do," "I am because I can be useful." Just as being can find substitute satisfaction through belonging, it can also take substitute satisfaction through ownership—as pointed out in the title of one of Erich Fromm's books: *To Have or To Be*.[2]

On the whole, the physical and obvious afford the Sancho Panzas of the world a most satisfying "ontic pacifier," and the search for being in the concrete, seeming most common-sensical, turns out to be the most hidden. Its hiddenness reminds us of Nasruddin's donkey: It is told that Nasruddin was seen at a remote outpost of customs officials crossing the border again and again on his donkey; he was suspected of smuggling something, but never were the customs inspectors able to find other than hay in his donkey's bags. When one of them ran into Nasruddin much later in life, at a time when both lived in a different country and had left behind the circumstances of their past, he asked the Mulla what it was that he was surely smuggling so astutely that they were never able to catch him for it. Nasruddin's answer was: donkeys.

While in its highest sense a pointer towards the hiddenness of God ("closer than our jugular vein") Nasruddin's smuggled donkey can also serve as a paradigm for the invisibility of ignorance and for the singular unobtrusiveness of ennea-type IX neurosis.

[2] Erich Fromm, *To Have or To Be* (New York: Bantam Books, Inc., 1982).

Chapter Ten

SUGGESTIONS FOR FURTHER WORK ON SELF

For those who are not part of an experiential teaching situation or a community, and yet want individually to put to work the information I have presented, it may be well to remember that spiritual progress occurs at an interface between what we can do (working from within our prison walls, so to speak) and what we allow to happen in an act of spiritual surrender and permeability. In other words, it is best not to become exclusively absorbed in "psychological work." Anybody who is not impermeable, who is not totally alienated from his full humanness will know in himself a capacity for a manner of remorse ("organic shame," to use E.J. Gold's expression) that lies beyond superegoic guilt in the face of worldly or other-worldly authority.

Just as, in Christian language, it is said that the acknowledgment of sin can be the gateway for contrition, purification, and eventual salvation, we may say in more contemporary terms that anyone who fully acknowledges psychological enslavement to the passions will feel a desire for liberation animated by the intuition of a spiritual freedom. In other words, he will intimately aspire or pray to be free of the passionate realm, so as to breathe loftier air.

Together with endorsing this wish for transformation and this turning from the world to the divine, I want to emphasize at the same time that the teaching strategy involved in this work is not only one of self-observational focus but includes the development of a neutrality vis-a-vis the study of the "machine," a neutrality in which the desire for change is not "acted out" in a precipitated and self-manipulative attempt to "perfect oneself."

Though behavior modification will be the focus of another stage in the inner work, this next stage of actively seeking the development of interpersonal virtue could hardly be tackled without the background of thorough self-awareness. Centuries of institutionalized do-goodism in all the higher civilizations clearly demonstrates that without self-understanding, self-intentional virtue can only be accomplished at the expense of repression and the impoverishment of consciousness.

When one practices the pursuit of self-knowledge in an attitude of prayerful aspiration and objective recognition of one's aberration, and yet at the same time seeks to make space in one's mind for such present imperfections as are unavoidable as a consequence of the imprints of past experience and the inevitable duration of the self-realization process, one comes to discover that self-understanding is sufficient to itself. Indeed the truth about ourselves can free us, for once we have truly understood something about ourselves, it will change without "our" attempt to change it. True insight into what we do and how and why we do it transforms our obsolete responses into idiocies which are likely to fall by the wayside or lose power over our essential intentions.

Whatever is valid in regard to awareness of our aberrations in general applies, of course, most pointedly to awareness of our chief feature and ruling passion, which involves the perception of the *gestalt* of one's many traits and their dynamic connection to these central foci.

In writing the nine preceding chapters I have implicitly assumed that the reader, coursing through them, will identify more with some characters than with others, and that for some of them self-recognition in the light of one particular set of traits and dynamics may come both spontaneously and effectively. Indeed, believing that the spelling-out of that character throughout the book can serve as a self-diagnostic instrument and also believing that knowledge of one's chief feature can make an individual free from its tyranny (as center of the psyche) make me feel very pleased.

For those who have not come to such self-recognition through reading the book alone, self-study oriented to an insight into their "chief feature" will remain as the most important aspect in the task of coming to know themselves better. Sometimes self-recognition is being resisted as a consequence of not having yet achieved the ripeness to see oneself objectively; in such cases insight will have to await this ripening, and the pursuit of self-recognition is likely to constitute a stimulus for acknowledging psychological realities as they are.

I advise those of my readers who have come to a realization of what the dominant passion is (and the corresponding fixation) to begin a course of additional self-study through the writing of an autobiography, that takes into account such insights. This auto-biography should include early memories—particularly the memories of painful situations and experiences in early family life; and it should become clear how, throughout the story of childhood, character was formed; particularly, how it was formed *as a way of coping* vis-a-vis painful circumstances.

To those who have come this far in following my suggestions, I recommend that they seek to immerse themselves in their memories as they write, and to make sure that their narration does not lapse into abstractions, but that it reflects the sounds, the sights, the recollected actions, attitudes and feelings of the past. Don't hurry, but welcome the opportunity to be in touch with your memories for whatever time it takes.

When immersing yourself in your experience of the past, seek to cultivate the attitude of an impartial observer. Write as one who merely *reports* on the facts, inner experiences, thoughts, decisions, actions, or reactions of the past. After the story of childhood, observe both your growth and your ego-growth during adolescence, a time when the pain of childhood becomes conscious of itself, a time when the yearning for what was missing in childhood gives shape to the earliest dreams and life projects. After this, as you continue with your life story, you may observe the living-out of these early dreams or ideals.

Make out of the writing of this autobiography a study in the origins and development of your particular character—centered on your particular ruling passion and fixation. When you finish analysing your past, in terms of this basic structure, you will be in a better position to observe your "machine" in ordinary life and in the here and now.

After the study of your past life, you will be prepared to undertake an ongoing self-analysis from the point of view of these ideas—i.e. an ongoing self-administered Protoanalysis: the processing of daily experience in the light of the psychological understanding discussed in this book. This will involve the discipline of self-observation and also a discipline of retrospection—a chewing-up of recent experience in the light of "work ideas."

Since a relevant work idea, in connection with this discipline, is the recognition of the particular usefulness of attending to "negative emotions," and, since these are painful states caused by the frustration of the passions, it may be said that an inevitable aspect of this work is what Gurdjieff used to call "conscious suffering"—a willingness to stay with such experiences as need to be observed and investigated.

The ideal material to process in one's writing is that of painful and unsatisfactory moments in the day: moments of frustration, guilt, fear, hurt, pride, solitude, and so on. In particular, examine episodes that may be felt as "wrongly lived": times when one feels that one's behavior or words were not what they could have been, and one looks for an alternative, wishing to "re-write" the episode in one's life. It is to these that one should begin to apply the book's information, seeking for the operation of the passion—one's ruling passion, in particular—and seeking also to identify the traits or attitudes, linking this behavior to one's generalized way of being.

In addition to the ongoing writing-up of painful interpersonal episodes and their analysis, one should seek to include more and more the experience of existential pain: i.e., the pain of feeling (perhaps increasingly) one's mechanicalness, the conditioned nature of one's personality, one's lack of ultimate reality and, especially, the lack of a sense of truly being.

We might say that the ordinary condition of the mind is half full and half empty in regard to the sense of being. We are only half conscious of our unconsciousness, only half aware of our disconnection with what should be the core of a human being's experience. Or rather, we might say that we have obscured an old, too-painful sense of existential vacuum with a false sense of being, that is supported in the various illusions peculiar to each character.

Awareness of endarkenment is the deepest aspect of conscious suffering—yet burning in this pain, for anyone who plunges into it, is the source of the most

precious fuel for the work of transformation. I would
recommend to those who have thus applied themselves
to self-observation and journal writing for 3 or 4 months
to re-read what I have written under the heading of
"existential psycho-dynamics" (in the chapters corresponding to their ego types) and that, drawing on
their observations, they write a statement of both
corroboration and amplification.

Work of self-observation such as I have been
recommending is not only an occasion for the
development of an observing self, which is an intrinsic
aspect of progress along the path of self-knowledge;
growth of the capacity to be a witness of oneself, in
turn, is a factor that supports the harvesting of
psychological insight.

Of the various disciplines used to develop a
self-aware, non-robotic, and centered stance, I particularly recommend, as a beginning, the task of
ongoing belly-centered awareness as described by
Karlfried von Dürckheim in his book *Hara*, to the
reading of which I can refer the sufficiently interested
practitioner for further inspir..tion.[1] Essentially, the
practice consists in maintaining throughout daily life a
sense of presence at a point about four fingers under
the navel, coupled with abdominal relaxation,
relaxation of the shoulders, alignment of the body axis
to gravity, and breathing aw.reness.

An additional recommendation to those who share
an interest in continuing to use this book beyond its
reading, is to further develop their ability to experience
the moment without conceptualization or judgement,
which may be done through the practice of *vipassana*
meditation.

The combination of self-study and meditation has
been one of the constant features of my work, and the

---

[1] Karlfried Graf von Dürckheim, *Hara: The Vital Centre of Man*,
(London: George Allen and Unwin, Ltd,. 1962).

natural consequence of a schooling in both Buddhism and the "Fourth Way." After nearly 20 years of experimentation, I have come to the conviction that the most suitable background for Protoanalysis proper is that of *vipassana*, with particular emphasis on the mindfulness of sensations and emotions, while the practice of *samatha*, with its emphasis on tranquility, is the most appropriate for the second stage of the work—where the focus is on behavior and development of the virtues.

A number of books on *vipassana* are in print and may serve both as a stimulus and a basis for wider understanding of the topic, yet I'll finish this set of suggested prescriptions with the following *vipassana* instructions that may be put in practice from this very day on:

- Sit, either on a chair or, preferably, in the half-lotus posture or on a meditation bench.

- Close your eyes and relax. Relax your shoulders, in particular be sure you relax your tongue—more connected to internal dialogues than is usually realized. Let your body hang from your spine and sink, if possible, into your belly. Relax your hands and feet, too.

- Attend to your breath, now.

- Allow your internal animal to do the breathing, if possible, or your lower brain—rather than telling yourself to breathe in and to breathe out in a military fashion.

- Now, add the awareness of the rising and falling of your upper abdomen to the awareness needed to drop muscle tensions and to be in touch with your breathing. Seek actually to sense the abdominal wall at the epigastrium (i.e. the triangular region under the tip of the sternum and between the descending lower ribs) as it rises and falls within each breathing cycle. Be in touch with your "solar-plexus" as your abdominal wall rises and falls with each breathing cycle.

While the above may be sufficient practice for several meditation sessions, it is only a back-bone of *vipassana* practice proper. Once you have attempted it and developed some proficiency at it, regard your breathing as a reminder to ask yourself, with every in-breath the question "what do I experience now?" In this manner, the meditation exercise becomes one of an ongoing awareness of mental events without forgetfulness of the breath or of the abdominal focus.

The question "what do I experience now?" need not be put in words, of course. The very act of breathing can be taken as the equivalent of a wordless question, or a wordless reminder to be in touch with whatever is happening in the body, feelings, and subtler aspects of the mind.

While the above corresponds to contemporary attempts in psychotherapy to be in touch with the "here and now," the distinctive characteristic of *vipassana* practice is a *particular attitude* toward ongoing experience: a centered attitude, comparable to that which we have discussed in connection with the awareness of daily life; a *neutral* attitude of making space for whatever is there, an attitude of panoramic availability of attention. More deeply, yet, it is an attitude of not grasping for anything and not rejecting anything—an attitude of openness and non-attached equanimity.

BIOGRAPHICAL NOTE

Claudio Naranjo, M.D., studied medicine and music at the University of Chile and the Chilean National Conservatory of Music, served residency at the University Clinic and contributed to the direction and activities of the Department of Anthropological Medicine of the medical school. He also taught social psychiatry in Chile at the School of Education and psychology of art at the Catholic University.

Dr. Naranjo has been a pioneer in psychological research and innovative techniques from the outset of his career. While teaching in Chile, he conducted psychopharmacological research that led to the introduction of various psychotropic drugs (such as yage, ibogaine, and MDA) into clinical practice. In consultation with Dr. Raymond Cattell he established in 1963 a South American branch of the Institute of Personality and Ability Testing and conducted factor analytic work leading to cross-cultural studies in personality structure and the creation of psychological diagnostic instruments.

He underwent training analysis at the Chilean Institute of Psychoanalysis, an intensive self-analysis under a Karen Horney-trained therapist, gestalt therapy with Fritz Perls and Dr. James Simkin. Naranjo was later a Fullbright Visiting Scholar at the Department of Social Relations at Harvard, at the University of Illinois,

Urbana, and at the University of California, Berkeley, conducting research on the psychology of values. He also taught at the Institute of Asian Studies, at Nyingma Institute and at the University of California, Santa Cruz. As a research associate at University of California's Institute of Personality Assessment and Research, he contributed to various research projects and wrote several books, including *The Psychology of Meditation*, in collaboration with Dr. Robert Ornstein, and *The One Quest*, among the earliest books to present a psychological perspective of the traditional spiritual paths.

Aside from his extensive contributions in research and teaching (and his own therapeutic practice with individuals), Claudio Naranjo is widely acknowledged as a co-sponsor of the original Arica training given by Oscar Ichazo to a group of American professionals and doctors, as narrated in Dr. John Lilly's autobiographical *Center of the Cyclone*. He is credited with the brilliant adaptation of the enneagram teaching, derived from esoteric sources in the Middle East, to contemporary psychology and psychiatric practice. It was Naranjo's teaching in the Berkeley area that initiated most of the therapists and authors who have since published books on the uses of the enneagram of personality types. In 1971, he founded SAT Institute, an integrative psychospiritual school now located in Andalucia, Spain.

Over the years, Dr. Naranjo has been a keynote speaker for the Association for Humanistic Psychology and the European Association for Humanistic Psychology, and at several national and international Gestalt and Transpersonal Psychology Conferences. He is a member of the U.S. Club of Rome, he is on the editorial board of the Journal of Humanistic Psychology, Honorary Director of the Gestalt Institute of Chile, and a fellow of the Institute for Cultural Research, London. Dr. Naranjo's recent books include *How to Be* (Jeremy S. Tarcher, Inc.), *Techniques of Gestalt Therapy* (Gestalt Journal) and *La Vieja y Novissima Gestalt* (Quatrovientos).

OUTLINE OF ENNEA-TYPE STRUCTURES

Chapter One: Angry Virtue (Ennea-Type I)
    1. Anger and Perfectionism
    2. Trait Structure
        Anger
        Criticality
        Demandingness
        Dominance
        Perfectionism
        Over-Control
        Self-Criticism
        Discipline
    3. Existential Psychodynamics

Chapter Two: Egocentric Generosity (Ennea-type II)
    1. Pride and Histrionism
    2. Trait Structure
        Pride
        Love Need
        Hedonism
        Seductiveness
        Assertiveness
        Nurturance and False Abundance,
        Histrionism
        Impressionable Emotionality
    3. Existential Psychodynamics

Chapter Three: Success through Appearances (Ennea-type III)

    1. Vanity, Inauthenticity and the "Marketing Orientation"

    2. Trait Structure

        Attention Need and Vanity

        Achieving Orientation

        Social Sophistication and Skill

        Cultivation of Sexual Attractiveness

        Deceit and Image Manipulation

        Other-Directedness

        Pragmatism

        Active Vigilance

        Superficiality

    3. Existential Psychodynamics

Chapter Four: Seeking Happiness through Pain (Ennea-type IV)

    1. Envy and the Masochistic Personality

    2. Trait Structure

        Envy

        Poor Self-Image

        Focus on Suffering

        "Moving Toward"

        Nurturance

        Emotionality

        Competitive Arrogance

        Refinement

        Artistic Interests

        Strong Superego

    3. Existential Psychodynamics

Chapter Seven

Opportunistic Idealism (Ennea-type VII)
1. Gluttony, Fraudulence and Narcissism
2. Trait Structure
Gluttony
HedonisticPermissiveness
Rebelliousness
Lack of Discipline
Imaginary Wish Fulfillment
Seductive Pleasingness
Narcissism
Persuasiveness
Fraudulence
3. Existential Psychodynamics

Chapter Eight

Coming on Strong (Ennea-type VIII)
1. Lust and Vindictive Arrogance
2. Trait Structure
Lust
Punitiveness
Rebelliousness
Dominance
Insensitivity
Conning and Cynicism
Exhibitionism(Narcissism)
Autonomy
Sensorimotor Dominance
3. Existential Psychodynamics

Chapter Nine: Going with the Stream (Ennea-type IX)

Dear Reader of *Ennea-type Structures*,

For a current catalog, including a variety of books, audio, and video recordings of Claudio Naranjo, you may contact Gateways at the address below with no obligation to purchase.

Gateways Books and Tapes
P.O. Box 370-ENS
Nevada City, CA 95959
(800) 869-0658 or (530) 477-8101
www.gatewaysbooksandtapes.com
email: info@gatewaysbooksandtapes.com

**Other Gateways Consciousness Classics
by Claudio Naranjo:**

**Enneagram of Society:
Healing the Soul to Heal the World**
Claudio Naranjo is finally awakening the spiritual world to its social conscience.

—E.J. Gold
Author of *Practical Work on Self, American Book of the Dead*

**The Divine Child and the Hero:
Inner Meaning in Children's Literature**
In writing this book, Claudio Naranjo has submitted himself to what the I-Ching calls "The Taming Power of the Small." I feel certain that his eight authors, whether they are in this world or in Heaven, will salute Dr. Naranjo for this perceptive essay.
—from the preface by P.L. Travers, author of *Mary Poppins*